WHAT THE CONFEDERATE FLAG MEANS TO ME

∞ THE LOCHLAINN SEABROOK COLLECTION ∞

AMERICAN CIVIL WAR
Abraham Lincoln Was a Liberal, Jefferson Davis Was a Conservative: The Missing Key to Understanding the American Civil War
Confederacy 101: Amazing Facts You Never Knew About America's Oldest Political Tradition
Confederate Blood and Treasure: An Interview With Lochlainn Seabrook
Everything You Were Taught About African-Americans and the Civil War is Wrong, Ask a Southerner!
Everything You Were Taught About the Civil War is Wrong, Ask a Southerner!
Give This Book to a Yankee! A Southern Guide to the Civil War For Northerners
Heroes of the Southern Confederacy: The Illustrated Book of Confederate Officials, Soldiers, and Civilians
Lincoln's War: The Real Cause, the Real Winner, the Real Loser
The Great Yankee Coverup: What the North Doesn't Want You to Know About Lincoln's War!
The Ultimate Civil War Quiz Book: How Much Do You Really Know About America's Most Misunderstood Conflict?
Women in Gray: A Tribute to the Ladies Who Supported the Southern Confederacy

CONFEDERATE MONUMENTS
Confederate Monuments: Why Every American Should Honor Confederate Soldiers and Their Memorials

CONFEDERATE FLAG
Confederate Flag Facts: What Every American Should Know About Dixie's Southern Cross
What the Confederate Flag Means to Me: Americans Speak Out in Defense of Southern Honor, Heritage, and History

SECESSION
All We Ask Is To Be Let Alone: The Southern Secession Fact Book

SLAVERY
Everything You Were Taught About American Slavery is Wrong, Ask a Southerner!
Slavery 101: Amazing Facts You Never Knew About America's "Peculiar Institution"

CHILDREN
Honest Jeff and Dishonest Abe: A Southern Children's Guide to the Civil War
Saddle, Sword, and Gun: A Biography of Nathan Bedford Forrest For Teens

NATHAN BEDFORD FORREST
A Rebel Born: A Defense of Nathan Bedford Forrest - Confederate General, American Legend (winner of the 2011 Jefferson Davis Historical Gold Medal)
A Rebel Born: The Screenplay (film about N. B. Forrest)
Forrest! 99 Reasons to Love Nathan Bedford Forrest
Give 'Em Hell Boys! The Complete Military Correspondence of Nathan Bedford Forrest
I Rode With Forrest! Confederate Soldiers Who Served With the World's Greatest Cavalry Leader
Nathan Bedford Forrest and African-Americans: Yankee Myth, Confederate Fact
Nathan Bedford Forrest and the Battle of Fort Pillow: Yankee Myth, Confederate Fact
Nathan Bedford Forrest and the Ku Klux Klan: Yankee Myth, Confederate Fact
Nathan Bedford Forrest: Southern Hero, American Patriot - Honoring a Confederate Icon and the Old South
Saddle, Sword, and Gun: A Biography of Nathan Bedford Forrest For Teens
The God of War: Nathan Bedford Forrest As He Was Seen By His Contemporaries
The Quotable Nathan Bedford Forrest: Selections From the Writings and Speeches of the Confederacy's Most Brilliant Cavalryman

QUOTABLE SERIES
The Alexander H. Stephens Reader: Excerpts From the Works of a Confederate Founding Father
The Quotable Alexander H. Stephens: Selections From the Writings and Speeches of the Confederacy's First Vice President
The Quotable Jefferson Davis: Selections From the Writings and Speeches of the Confederacy's First President
The Quotable Nathan Bedford Forrest: Selections From the Writings and Speeches of the Confederacy's Most Brilliant Cavalryman
The Quotable Robert E. Lee: Selections From the Writings and Speeches of the South's Most Beloved Civil War General
The Quotable Stonewall Jackson: Selections From the Writings and Speeches of the South's Most Famous General
The Unquotable Abraham Lincoln: The President's Quotes They Don't Want You To Know!

CIVIL WAR BATTLES
Encyclopedia of the Battle of Franklin - A Comprehensive Guide to the Conflict that Changed the Civil War
Nathan Bedford Forrest and the Battle of Fort Pillow: Yankee Myth, Confederate Fact
The Battle of Franklin: Recollections of Confederate and Union Soldiers
The Battle of Nashville: Recollections of Confederate and Union Soldiers
The Battle of Spring Hill: Recollections of Confederate and Union Soldiers

CONSTITUTIONAL HISTORY
America's Three Constitutions: Complete Texts of the Articles of Confederation, Constitution of the United States of America, and Constitution of the Confederate States of America
The Articles of Confederation Explained: A Clause-by-Clause Study of America's First Constitution
The Constitution of the Confederate States of America Explained: A Clause-by-Clause Study of the South's Magna Carta

VICTORIAN CONFEDERATE LITERATURE
Rise Up and Call Them Blessed: Victorian Tributes to the Confederate Soldier, 1861-1901
Support Your Local Confederate: Wit and Humor in the Southern Confederacy
The God of War: Nathan Bedford Forrest As He Was Seen By His Contemporaries
The Old Rebel: Robert E. Lee As He Was Seen By His Contemporaries
Victorian Confederate Poetry: The Southern Cause in Verse, 1861-1901

ABRAHAM LINCOLN
Abraham Lincoln: The Southern View - Demythologizing America's Sixteenth President
Lincolnology: The Real Abraham Lincoln Revealed in His Own Words - A Study of Lincoln's Suppressed, Misinterpreted, and Forgotten Writings and Speeches
Lincoln's War: The Real Cause, the Real Winner, the Real Loser
The Great Impersonator! 99 Reasons to Dislike Abraham Lincoln
The Unholy Crusade: Lincoln's Legacy of Destruction in the American South
The Unquotable Abraham Lincoln: The President's Quotes They Don't Want You To Know!

NATURAL HISTORY
North America's Amazing Mammals: An Encyclopedia for the Whole Family
The Concise Book of Owls: A Guide to Nature's Most Mysterious Birds
The Concise Book of Tigers: A Guide to Nature's Most Remarkable Cats

PARANORMAL
Carnton Plantation Ghost Stories: True Tales of the Unexplained from Tennessee's Most Haunted Civil War House!
UFOs and Aliens: The Complete Guidebook

FAMILY HISTORIES
The Blakeneys: An Etymological, Ethnological, and Genealogical Study - Uncovering the Mysterious Origins of the Blakeney Family and Name
The Caudills: An Etymological, Ethnological, and Genealogical Study - Exploring the Name and National Origins of a European-American Family
The McGavocks of Carnton Plantation: A Southern History - Celebrating One of Dixie's Most Noble Confederate Families and Their Tennessee Home

MIND, BODY, SPIRIT
Autobiography of a Non-Yogi: A Scientist's Journey From Hinduism to Christianity (Dr. Amitava Dasgupta, with Lochlainn Seabrook)
Britannia Rules: Goddess-Worship in Ancient Anglo-Celtic Society - An Academic Look at the United Kingdom's Matricentric Spiritual Past
Christ Is All and In All: Rediscovering Your Divine Nature and the Kingdom Within
Christmas Before Christianity: How the Birthday of the "Sun" Became the Birthday of the "Son"
Jesus and the Gospel of Q: Christ's Pre-Christian Teachings As Recorded in the New Testament
Jesus and the Law of Attraction: The Bible-Based Guide to Creating Perfect Health, Wealth, and Happiness Following Christ's Simple Formula
Seabrook's Bible Dictionary of Traditional and Mystical Christian Doctrines
Sea Raven Press Blank Page Journal: For Reflections, Notes, and Sketches
The Bible and the Law of Attraction: 99 Teachings of Jesus, the Apostles, and the Prophets
The Book of Kelle: An Introduction to Goddess-Worship and the Great Celtic Mother-Goddess Kelle, Original Blessed Lady of Ireland
The Goddess Dictionary of Words and Phrases: Introducing a New Core Vocabulary for the Women's Spirituality Movement
The Martian Anomalies: Photographic Proof of Ancient Intelligent Life on Mars
Vintage Southern Cookbook: Delicious Dishes From Dixie

WOMEN
Aphrodite's Trade: The Hidden History of Prostitution Unveiled
Princess Diana: Modern Day Moon-Goddess - A Psychoanalytical and Mythological Look at Diana Spencer's Life, Marriage, and Death (with Dr. Jane Goldberg)
Women in Gray: A Tribute to the Ladies Who Supported the Southern Confederacy

REPRINTS
A Short History of the Confederate States of America (author Jefferson Davis; editor Lochlainn Seabrook)
Prison Life of Jefferson Davis (author John J. Craven; editor Lochlainn Seabrook)
Life of Beethoven (author Ludwig Nohl; editor Lochlainn Seabrook)
The New Revelation (author Arthur Conan Doyle; editor Lochlainn Seabrook)

Lochlainn Seabrook does not author books for fame and fortune, but for the love of writing and sharing his knowledge.

SeaRavenPress.com

Warning:
SEA RAVEN PRESS
BOOKS WILL EXPAND
YOUR ★ MIND!

WHAT THE
CONFEDERATE FLAG
MEANS TO ME

Americans Speak Out in Defense of
Southern Honor, Heritage, & History

COLLECTED, EDITED, & ARRANGED, WITH AN INTRODUCTION BY THE AUTHOR,
"THE VOICE OF THE TRADITIONAL SOUTH," COLONEL

LOCHLAINN SEABROOK

JEFFERSON DAVIS HISTORICAL GOLD MEDAL WINNER

Generously Illustrated and Captioned by
Col. Seabrook for the Elucidation of the Reader

2021

Sea Raven Press, Nashville, Tennessee, USA

Published by
Sea Raven Press, Cassidy Ravensdale, President
Nashville, Tennessee USA
SeaRavenPress.com • searavenpress@gmail.com

SEA RAVEN PRESS
SOUTHERN BOOKS, REAL HISTORY!

1ˢᵗ SRP paperback edition, 1ˢᵗ printing, February 2021 • ISBN: 978-1-943737-94-9
1ˢᵗ SRP hardcover edition, 1ˢᵗ printing, February 2021 • ISBN: 978-1-943737-95-6

ISBN: 978-1-943737-94-9 (paperback)
Library of Congress Control Number: 2021930220

What the Confederate Flag Means to Me: Americans Speak Out in Defense of Southern Honor,
Heritage, and History, by Lochlainn Seabrook. Includes color illustrations, an introduction, and an
index. Statements 1-16 and 18-33 published by permission of the commentators and are the
copyrighted property of Lochlainn Seabrook.

Front and back cover design and art, book design, layout, and interior art by Lochlainn Seabrook
All images, graphic design, graphic art, and illustrations copyright © Lochlainn Seabrook
All images selected, placed, manipulated, and/or created by Lochlainn Seabrook
Cover photo: Confederate Graves (unknown), Battle of Bentonville, Four Oaks, NC, Jim Hawthorn

SEA RAVEN PRESS

DEDICATION

To My Louisiana Cousin,
Confederate General Pierre Gustave Toutant Beauregard,
Who Zealously Loved the Design and Colors of the "Southern Cross"
and Who Was Instrumental in Establishing it as
the Confederacy's Official Battle Flag.

EPIGRAPH

When the Right learns the Truth about
the Confederate Battle Flag, it will be
flown from every Conservative's rooftop.

Lochlainn Seabrook
February 2021

CONTENTS

Notes to the Reader - 11
Introduction, by Lochlainn Seabrook - 15
An Assortment of Flags Bearing the Christian Cross - 33

ENTRIES
1. Al Benson Jr.: 39
2. Birch Bricker: 42
3. B. L. Reid: 46
4. Bobby Fears: 49
5. Chuck Johnson: 51
6. Doug Boren: 54
7. Gary Price: 57
8. Gil Luna: 60
9. Gloria Peoples-Elam: 63
10. James Johnson: 66
11. James Pierce: 69
12. Jason Prather: 71
13. J. Sanford Kruizenga: 73
14. Kevin J. Miller: 75
15. Kimberly Parker: 78
16. Kurt Schluchter: 80
17. Lochlainn Seabrook: 84
18. Michael and Julia Davis: 90
19. Patrick W. Merritt: 92
20. Percival Beacroft: 95
21. Robert Allen: 97
22. Robert Castello: 100

23. Robert M. Schwartz: 102

24. Sandra Griffith Fish: 104

25. Scott Bowden: 107

26. Stephen Kelley: 109

27. Steve Quick: 112

28. Thomas H. McFarland: 114

29. Tom Hamilton: 118

30. Tom Kopczak: 120

31. Wesley D. King: 122

32. W. G. Hardeman: 125

33. Woody W. Woodward: 127

Index - 129

Save the South: How You Can Help Protect Our Priceless Heritage - 135

Meet the Author-Editor - 147

NOTES TO THE READER

THE TWO MAIN POLITICAL PARTIES IN 1860

☛ Nothing in this book will make sense—indeed, nothing concerning the War for Southern Independence will make sense—without knowing that in 1860 the two major political parties, the Democrats and the newly formed Republicans, were the opposite of what they are today. In other words, the Democrats of the mid 19th Century were Conservatives, akin to the Republican Party of today, while the Republicans of the mid 19th Century were Liberals, akin to the Democratic Party of today.

The author's cousin, Confederate Vice President and Democrat Alexander H. Stephens: a Southern Conservative.

Thus the Confederacy's Democratic president, Jefferson Davis, was a Conservative (with libertarian leanings); the Union's Republican president, Abraham Lincoln, was a Liberal (with socialistic leanings).[1]

ORDER OF ENTRIES

☛ The entries in this book are listed alphabetically, by first name.

---

1. For a full discussion of these topics see my books: 1) *Lincoln's War: The Real Cause, The Real Winner, the Real Loser*. Spring Hill, TN: Sea Raven Press, 2016; 2) *Abraham Lincoln Was a Liberal, Jefferson Davis Was a Conservative: The Missing Key to Understanding the American Civil War*. Spring Hill, TN: Sea Raven Press, 2017; 3) *Abraham Lincoln: The Southern View*. 2007. Franklin, TN: Sea Raven Press, 2013 ed.

IMAGE QUALITY

☞ Many of the images in this book are from sources that are between 70 and 160 years old, making them inherently low resolution. As I prefer vintage illustrations for my works, this is intentional.

Conservative Confederate General Thomas Jonathan "Stonewall" Jackson. The venerable Christian Southerner gave his life in the fight against Left-wing tyranny, and thus will always be a hero in the eyes of true American patriots .

LEARN MORE

☞ The truth about the Confederate Battle Flag, as well as Lincoln's War on the Constitution and the American people, can never be fully understood without a thorough knowledge of the South's perspective. As this book is only meant to be a brief introductory guide to these topics, one cannot hope to learn the complete story here. For those who are interested in additional material from Dixie's viewpoint, please see my comprehensive histories listed on pages 2 and 3.

Liberals would like you to think that the facts about Lincoln's War are straightforward, simplistic, plain black and white. In reality, it was a profoundly intricate conflict, made even more so by the Left's complete rewriting of the War's history to suit their communist agenda. In my books I have sought to untangle the horrendous mess they have created with their illogical fake history (millions of men and women, for example, would not have risked their lives to either destroy or preserve slavery), and present the highly nuanced Truth in an easily comprehensible manner.

Loyalty

to the truth of

Confederate history.

U.D.C. MOTTO, 1921

INTRODUCTION

T HE CONFEDERATE BATTLE FLAG—or for our purposes the Confederate Flag for short—was a military banner used by a Conservative government, the Confederate States of America (1861-1865), which took up arms against the Liberal North (the Union) in an attempt to preserve the Constitution, a conservative document. Despite this simple fact of history, like all symbols, the Confederate Flag evokes a wide variety of beliefs, ideas, feelings, views, and emotions; which is why it means so many things to so many different people.

The CSS *Shenandoah* flying the 2nd National Flag, the official flag of the Confederate States of America from May 1, 1863, to March 4, 1865.

Adding to the diverse sentiment and confusion surrounding our beautiful ensign is that the flag itself has a convoluted vexillological history, as I discuss in detail in my book *Confederate Flag Facts*.[2]

The well-known "Southern Cross" design was first approved by Confederate officers Joseph E. Johnston and Pierre G. T. Beauregard September 1861, and formally issued for field use

---

2. Lochlainn Seabrook, *Confederate Flag Facts: What Every American Should Know About Dixie's Southern Cross*. Spring Hill, TN: Sea Raven Press, 2016.

November 1861. Henceforth its eye-catching X-shaped layout (based on Scotland's Saint Andrew's Flag) was used, in a myriad of shapes, sizes, and forms, by Confederate officers such as: Robert E. Lee (Army of Northern Virginia); Richard Taylor (Richard Taylor's Army); Joseph O. Shelby (Shelby's Brigade); (J. E.) Johnston and John Bell Hood (Army of Tennessee); Beauregard (Western Theater); Mosby M. Parsons (Parson's Texas Cavalry); and Braxton Bragg (Army of the Mississippi), among others.

Conservative Confederate General Joseph E. Johnston of Virginia was one of the first to appreciate and approve the now famous X-shaped battle flag design.

It also saw service as the battle flag of the Department of South Carolina, Georgia, and Florida, as well as the Department of Alabama, Mississippi, and East Louisiana. Notably, after May 26, 1863, it became the Confederacy's official Navy Jack, subsequently taking its place on the cantons of both the C.S. Second National Flag (the "Stainless Banner") and C.S. Third National Flag (the "Blood Stained Banner").

The first classic C.S. battle flag design—submitted to the Confederate Congress for consideration on March 4, 1861, by William Porcher Miles—sported seven stars, each representing one of the seven Southern states that had seceded at that point. As additional states left the Union more stars were added.

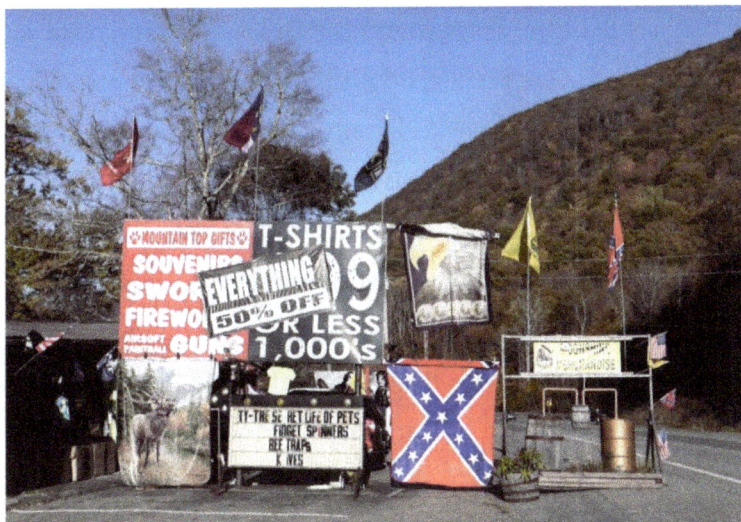

Confederate Battle Flags for sale from a roadside vendor, Smoky Mountain region of North Carolina, circa 2017.

A Confederate veteran presenting a Confederate Battle Flag wreath at Arlington, Virginia, circa 1920. It reads: "CSA '61-'65."

Nathan Bedford Forrest and his famous cavalry rode into battle with a 12 star battle flag, one he used for most of the war for sentimental reasons.[3] Eventually it came to be the magnificent 13 star banner we are so familiar with today.[4]

The Confederate Battle Flag survived into modern times on the state flags of Georgia and Mississippi (both now removed and replaced), and, as the red diagonal Saint Patrick's Cross, on the state flags of Florida and Alabama.

Conservative Confederate Congressman William Porcher Miles of South Carolina: Chairman of the C.S.A.'s Committee on Flag and Seal, and the enthusiastic designer of the classic Confederate Battle Flag.

While its labyrinthian history and countless uses have tended to obscure the original meaning of the Confederate Battle Flag, this is not what caused it to become a "symbol of hate" to the simple minded, the intolerant, the vindictive, and the uneducated. It was the angry, miserable, emotionally immature, political Left who reprehensibly, purposefully, and "with malice toward all," distorted, rewrote, and suppressed the truth about our Starry Cross.

As part of its plan to overthrow the United States government, the radical Left (socialists, communists, anarchists, etc.), has demonized, and continues to demonize, everything traditionally American. This, of course, includes the

---

3. Learn the truth about General Forrest: see my 12 books on the man for whom there are not enough superlatives.
4. For more on the topic of secession and the formation of the Confederacy see my book, *All We Ask is to be Let Alone: The Southern Secession Fact Book*. Spring Hill, TN: Sea Raven Press, 2017.

Conservative American South and all that she holds dear: her history, culture, heritage, customs, land, symbols, statuary, art, cemeteries, and memorabilia.[5]

The process of vilifying the South was well underway long before the War Between the States. Writing in the late 1700s and early 1800s, Southern Conservative Thomas Jefferson, for example, made countless references to the sociopolitical tension between the Liberal North and the Conservative South,[6] a condition that only grew more obvious and severe in the following decades. As prewar sentiment began to swell in early 1861, Yankee Leftists were already busy churning out one falsehood after another in order to mislead the public and gain political leverage over Dixie.[7]

Over 200 years ago Conservative Virginian and U.S. President Thomas Jefferson frequently commented on the growing tension between the South and the North, even accurately predicting a future war between the political Left (Yankees) and the political Right (Confederates) that would entail "rivers of blood."

At the head of this movement to discredit the South and destroy her culture was Abraham Lincoln, a Left-wing atheistic megalomaniac who surrounded himself with socialists and communists, many of them personal friends of the infamous founder of modern communism, Karl Marx.[8]

---

5. For more on the suppressed facts about the South see my book, *The Great Yankee Coverup: What the North Doesn't Want You to Know About Lincoln's War!* Spring Hill, TN: Sea Raven Press, 2015.
6. See, for example, Merrill D. Peterson, ed., *Thomas Jefferson: Writings*, New York: Literary Classics, 1984, pp. 684, 972, 988-989, 1049, 1050, 1078-1079, 1087, 1448, 1478.
7. I discuss these falsehoods in great detail in my book, *Everything You Were Taught About the Civil War is Wrong, Ask a Southerner!* 2010. Franklin, TN: Sea Raven Press, revised 2019 ed.
8. For a full discussion on Lincoln and the then Left-wing Republican Party and Jefferson Davis and the then Right-wing Democratic Party of the 1860s see my book, *Abraham Lincoln Was a Liberal, Jefferson Davis Was a Conservative: The Missing Key to Understanding the American Civil War*. Spring Hill, TN: Sea Raven Press, 2017.

While the modern Left busies itself with divisive tactics meant to engender continuing enmity between the South and the North, in reality most Confederate and Union veterans of Lincoln's War were anxious for peace and renewed brotherhood. This albumen print, for instance, created at Richmond, Virginia, July 5, 1887, is captioned "Meeting of the Blue and the Gray." The photo shows Union veteran Timothy S. Lee (left) of Co. C, 61st Massachusetts Infantry Regiment and Confederate veteran James Hannon (right) of Co. 1, 4th Virginia Cavalry Regiment, posing in front of a Confederate Battle Flag with Confederate General Robert E. Lee's portrait in the center. The Union vet was a member of the General Frederick West Lander Post (Massachusetts Post No. 5), G.A.R., while the Confederate vet was a member of the United Confederate Veterans (U.C.V.), R. E. Lee Camp, No. 1. Descriptive text accompanying the photograph relates that "in the presence of the survivors of the great struggle," the two men "clasped hands in brotherly love and reunion over the momentous past." Sadly, because peace and harmony would jeopardize their communist agenda to violently overthrow the U.S. government, the far Left will continue to try to prevent healing and unification between South and North. Demonization of the Confederate Battle Flag is only the first step. Everything will be employed in an attempt to keep the two sections in a permanent state of strife, tension, and bitterness. How? Through the Left's use of fake history, along with its fake outrage, fake race war, fake social war, and fake economic war. Besides gaslighting, one of its primary weapons in this battle is, and always has been, projection: a psychological mechanism in which one imbues others with his or her own traits, ideas, feelings, and beliefs (usually negative). Thus, the South-loather projects his or her own racism, self-hatred, ignorance, bigotry, intolerance, etc., onto the Confederacy. But there was nothing negative about the Conservative Christian C.S.A. The communist methods of what I call the *disinformation merchants* are easily exposed.

The primary weapons employed by the Victorian Left were the same tried and true communist tactics that are used today, and which have been in practice since at least the late 1840s, when Marx and Friedrich Engels published their anti-capitalist document, *The Communist Manifesto*. Declaring that the radical Left's goals can only be attained by "the forcible overthrow of all existing social conditions," the racist, bigoted, violent, and nihilistic concepts of Marx and Engels were further refined by 20th-Century communists during World War I (1914-1918), culminating, in a terse list of "Communist Rules for Bringing About a Revolution."

MANIFESTO
of the
COMMUNIST PARTY

BY
KARL MARX and FREDERICK ENGELS

AUTHORIZED ENGLISH TRANSLATION: EDITED AND
ANNOTATED BY FREDERICK ENGELS

CHICAGO
CHARLES H. KERR & COMPANY
1906

Cover of Marx's and Engel's anti-American (and thus anti-South) *Manifesto of the Communist Party*, 1906 edition.

For those who are not familiar with how the far Left operates, we will examine an alleged document containing these very instructions, one said to have been discovered by Allied Forces at Dusseldorf, Germany, in May 1919. According to one patriotic American commentator, the rules vividly "show the strategy of materialistic revolution, and how personal attitudes and habits of living affect the affairs of nations."[9]

---

9. *New World News*, February 1946.

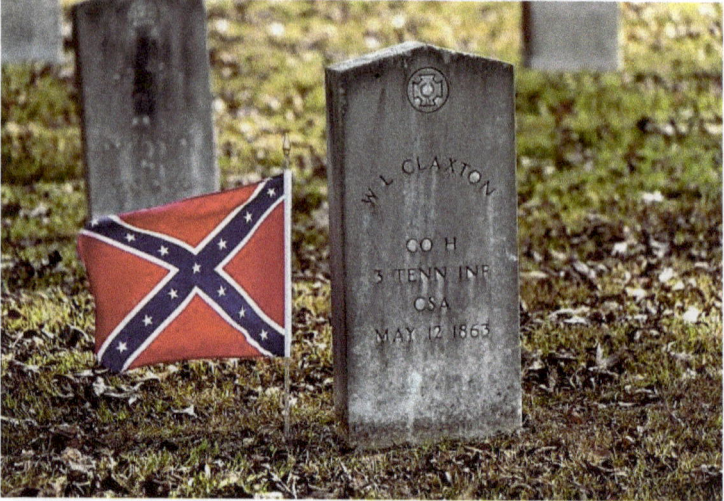

The grave of W. L. Claxton, Co. H, 3rd Tennessee Infantry, C.S.A.; one of the many Confederate soldiers who perished at the Battle of Raymond, May 12, 1863. Photo year: 2016. Location: Confederate Cemetery, Raymond, Mississippi.

A group of women reading the epitaphs of some of the Confederate dead on the gravestones at a cemetery in Charleston, South Carolina, circa 1903. For giving their lives for the Southern Cause (Conservatism), the names of these valiant men will be immortally engraved on the hearts of all true American patriots.

To achieve their end of bringing down the U.S. government and replacing it with a communist dictatorship, this short article instructs its revolutionary adherents to do the following:

A. Corrupt the young. Get them away from religion. Get them interested in sex. Make them superficial, destroy their ruggedness.

B. Get control of all means of publicity and thereby:

1. Take people's minds off their government by focusing their attention on athletics, books stressing sex, plays and other trivialities.

2. Divide the people into hostile groups by constantly harping on controversial matters of little or no importance.

3. Destroy the people's faith in their natural leaders by holding the latter up to contempt, ridicule, and disgrace.

4. Always "preach" true democracy, but seize power as fast and as ruthlessly as possible.

5. By encouraging government extravagance, destroy its credit and produce fear of inflation with rising prices and general discontent.

6. Incite unnecessary strikes in vital industries; encourage civil disorders and foster a lenient and soft attitude on the part of the government toward such disorders.

7. By specious arguments cause the breakdown of the old moral virtues: honesty, serious-mindedness, self-restraint, and faith in the pledged word.

C. Cause the registration of all firearms on some pretext, with a view to confiscating them at a later date, thereby leaving the population helpless.[10]

Each of these instructions is currently being used by American communists to undermine our Republic. How successful they have been is all too obvious to anyone over the age of 50.

Communism, and by association, leftism, liberalism, and socialism in general, operate, in great part, by gaslighting; that is, by introducing and feeding false information to an individual or group that makes them question their perception of reality, their memories, and even their sanity. Gaslighting manifests in many forms, but comes primarily through the dissemination of lies, propaganda, misinformation, and

The purpose of gaslighting—in this case by the political Left—is absolute control. Its intent is similar in nature, in fact, to the marionettist, who manipulates his or her puppet from above using wires and strings.

disinformation, all geared toward emotional manipulation. The gaslighter, proficient in the psychological torment and abuse of others, treats his or her untruths as factual—even though they are fully aware that it is all mental fakery, designed to frighten, injure, demoralize, and weaken their victims, divide their opponents, and confuse their followers. These methods, in

---

10. See *Hearings Before a Subcommittee of the Committee on Appropriations*, U.S. House of Representatives, 91st Congress, 1st Session, 1969, pp. 578-579; and the *U.S. Congressional Record* (Senate), Vol. 115, Pt. 18, August 13, 1969, p. 23698.

turn, are meant to not only erode tradition, but foment social, political, and racial strife and discord, opening the door for the introduction and installation of socialism, and later communism.

In pursuit of its nefarious goals, the intolerant hate-filled Left has inflicted some of its most spectacular damage in the area of American history. Not only by using such standard practices as the "Communist Rules for Bringing About a Revolution," but also by borrowing overt gaslighting techniques from the world of performance magic. These include all of the standard tools of the magician's trade: direction, misdirection, deception, ambiguity, perception bias, illusion, distraction, mental manipulation, conjuring, expectation alteration, sleight of hand, secrecy, psychological exploitation, ignorance exploitation, memory exploitation, cognitive exploitation, assumption manipulation, decision manipulation, belief susceptibility, surprise, shock, forcing techniques, pseudo psychological methods, fraud, lying, reality distortion, and outright trickery. (Careful observation will reveal all.)

The Left makes up only a minority of the U.S.A. Thus, if it did not rely on such techniques as gaslighting, cheating, lying, intimidation, violence, projection, disinformation, and standard magic tricks, it would be unable to either attain or retain power.

It is these same time-tested gaslighting methods that have been employed by the Left in completely reworking and revising the history of United States of America, including all of her wars and political events, from before the signing of our Constitution into the present day. Not one detail has been overlooked; not one person or event or symbol has ever been considered too insignificant to twist, taint, falsify, or weaponize. In this way, under the poisonous pen of the communist "historian," the true histories of entire nations have been rewritten, wars revised, biographies redacted. In the process, communists have cunningly presented reality as offensive and what was once offensive as reality. Hence, most of the true facts of American history are now unknown, distorted beyond recognition, suppressed and buried under mountains of anti-American, anti-capitalist, anti-Christian communist propaganda.[11]

German communist Karl Marx (many of whose personal friends and associates worked in the Lincoln administration and the Union military) unleashed a movement that helped bring down the Conservative Southern Confederacy in 1865, and which, 160 years later, is still pursuing the destruction of Dixie. Marx's socialist-flavored November 1864 letter to Lincoln (congratulating him on his reelection) was not happenstance.

Yet, due to the powerful "magical" qualities of gaslighting, few have noticed these sweeping alterations. In his novel *1984*, 20th-Century English writer George Orwell warned of a future in which the concept of objective fact would disappear and lies would pass into history as truth. We are indeed living in a *post-truth* world, a term which the dictionary defines as "relating to or existing in an environment in which facts are viewed as irrelevant, or less important than personal beliefs and opinions, and emotional appeals are used to influence public opinion."

---

11. I have chronicled and compiled massive evidence for the Left's revision of Southern history in my books; titles such as: *Everything You Were Taught About American Slavery is Wrong, Ask a Southerner!* Spring Hill, TN: Sea Raven Press, 2015, and *Everything You Were Taught About African-Americans and the Civil War is Wrong, Ask a Southerner!* Spring Hill, TN: Sea Raven Press, 2016.

Conservative women have always been among the Confederacy's strongest supporters. This group from the early 20th Century is holding up a Confederate Third National Flag. In front of them, a wreath—made into the Starry Cross from the Confederate Battle Flag—sits on a small stand. The Confederacy and its symbols were widely accepted by the public at this time in American history. Today the Left is scheming to ensure that scenes like this cannot and do not occur again. The traditional Conservative Christian South, however, will never stop paying tribute to the Confederate Flag and the brave Southern patriots who fought and died for the Conservative ideals it embodies.

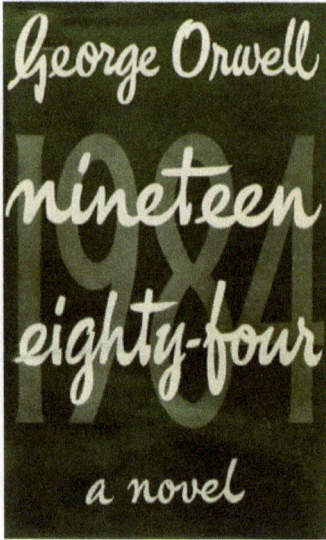

The 1949 cover of Orwell's popular prophetic book *1984*.

Many of us, however, *have* noticed the Left's lies becoming history, *fake* history, that is. Particularly Southern history. Unethically and incorrectly using presentism (judging our ancestors by today's very different standards), the Left has overturned the facts and even reversed them (another favorite progressive ploy), so that the beliefs, traditions, and symbols of the South are now deemed not only repugnant, but immoral and even malevolent.

As the primary emblem of the Conservative Christian South, the Confederate Battle Flag has, without question, suffered the most at the spiteful hands of the ignorant, the illiterate, and the indoctrinated. By demonizing the Southern Cross, as well as by rewriting both our history and the dictionary, the Left can now label everything Southern "racist," "treasonous," and "un-American." This (in their uncritical minds) gives them justification for restricting, outlawing, censoring, controlling, and criminalizing anything related to Dixie—their intention from the beginning. This has allowed them to, for example, ban the Confederate Flag from public property, curtail the sale and distribution of Confederate oriented books, movies, artwork, and photographs (like mine), and deface and remove

Confederate memorials, paintings, busts, and statues.[12]

Being a Confederate American and a Southern author I am probably more acutely aware than most of the extent to which the Confederate Flag has been manipulated by fact-detesting Big Tech (information technology industries), the South-hating Mainstream Media (Hollywood, TV, radio, pop culture, newspapers, book publishers), and in particular our Confederate-loathing federal government in Washington, D.C.

The U.S. Department of Education, which has been teaching our children a biased, South-shaming, purposefully inaccurate, communist propagandized version of the "Civil War" since 1865, is arguably the worst perpetrator in the latter category.

However, every U.S. governmental department has openly joined the crusade to obliterate both true American history and the South herself using various typical socialist and communist strategies. These include the Department of Agriculture, Department of Commerce,

The U.S. Federal Government easily outpaces every other American institution in anti-South propaganda, revisionism, rhetoric, and censorship. It long ago consigned the facts about Lincoln's War, the Confederates States of America, slavery, secession, and courageous Conservative patriots like Jefferson Davis, Alexander H. Stephens, Robert E. Lee, Stonewall Jackson, and Nathan Bedford Forrest (among many others), to the scrapheap of history. In place of the Truth, the U.S. government has manufactured and issued a completely fake history of the South—one approved by radical Left-wing "historians" and taught by socialist and communist "educators" to our children.

---

12. For a thorough examination of the topic of Confederate statues see my book, *Confederate Monuments: Why Every American Should Honor Confederate Soldiers and Their Memorials*. Spring Hill, TN: Sea Raven Press, 2018.

Department of Defense, Department of Energy, Department of Health and Human Services, Department of Homeland Security, Department of Housing and Urban Development, Department of Justice, Department of Labor, Department of State, Department of Transportation, Department of the Treasury, and the Department of Veterans Affairs. While in some cases quite subtle and even barely noticeable, South-hating, and the overt communism behind it, can be found in one form or another at all of these executive agencies.

The original Department of Interior building, Washington, D.C., circa 1870. While I am a U.S. patriot and a strong advocate of Americanism—and, as a lifelong outdoorsman, avidly support the work of the Department of the Interior in particular—I do not appreciate the Federal Government rewriting my region's history, deliberately sullying the names of my Confederate ancestors, and falsely portraying the C.S.A. as a "racist slavocracy." My books act as a small counterweight to the government's avalanche of biased disinformation, which is being disseminated to the American public in the name of education.

In particular must be made mention of the Department of the Interior, which operates the National Park Service, with a few minor exceptions, one of the most anti-historical, anti-South, anti-Confederate bodies in our government. U.S. agencies, branches, trusts, and government corporations that have taken public stances against the South and her symbols also include the Library of Congress, the Smithsonian Institution, and the U.S. Postal Service, to name just a few. To this list we must include most "Civil War" related houses, buildings, and battle sites across America (some owned by the government, some privately), nearly all which are

Liberal Lincoln's plans for Dixie were anything but benign. They included "obliterating" the Conservative agrarian South and remaking it in the image of the Liberal industrial North.

run by Leftists who have declared relentless war on the Confederate Battle Flag and the truth about the War for Southern Independence.

The Left's cultural Marxism—which includes its genocidal program to destroy the traditional South and her history—is not an accident, nor is it a product of true hatred for Dixie. The trashing of Southern history, along with the Northernization of the South, simply benefits the Left's primary cause: the conquest and transformation of the U.S.A. into a one-party socialist (and eventually communist) state. As noted, this is being accomplished in great part through agitation, the suppression of the facts, the censorship of pro-South authors and literature, and the wholesale redaction of American history. This is, of course, the realization of Lincoln's original dream.[13] As the Left-wing, Dixie-hating demagogue once commented to Interior Department official T. J. Barnett: "The entire South needs to be obliterated and replaced with new businessmen and new ideas."[14]

Notwithstanding the Liberals' all out war to demolish the South, her history, and her symbols, the objective Truth remains unchanged *and* accessible to those who have an open

---

13. For more on Lincoln and his Left-wing beliefs, policies, activities, administration, and army see my many books on America's 16th president (listed on pages 2 and 3).
14. Lochlainn Seabrook, *Abraham Lincoln: The Southern View*. 2007. Franklin, TN: Sea Raven Press, 2013 ed., p. 530.

curious mind; to those who have not yet succumb to the Left-wing's massive propaganda campaign to wipe out the South.[15]

By taking the time to write and submit their thoughts, the kind commentators in this book are helping to preserve the facts about a wonderful patriotic heritage; one that belongs to all Americans—and in particular, Conservative, Christian, Southern Americans *of all races*; one symbolized now and forever by the Confederate Flag, to us, the world's most beautiful and sacred banner.

The current but ridiculous idea that the Confederate Flag is a "hate symbol" is a communist invention, pure and simple. In one sense it is actually an anti-communist symbol, just one of the many real reasons the Left dislikes it.

Our unique military ensign, with its bold white starred blue cross on a deep red field, is not just a piece of cloth. It is possessed of sacred properties, enigmatic forces, and mysterious powers: In the 1860s millions of courageous Conservative men and women confederated under it and withdrew from a corrupt, un-American, ungodly Union.[16] Some day we will rally round it once again.

In the Bonds of the South,
LOCHLAINN SEABROOK
Nashville, Davidson County, Tennessee
February 2021

---

15. For a full examination of the War see my book, *Lincoln's War: The Real Cause, the Real Winner, the Real Loser*. Spring Hill, TN: Sea Raven Press, 2016.
16. For more on how the Confederate soldier was viewed by Southerners (and others) see my book, *Rise Up and Call Them Blessed: Victorian Tributes to the Confederate Soldier, 1861-1901*. Spring Hill, TN: Sea Raven Press, 2017.

An Assortment of Flags Bearing the Christian Cross

C.S.A. Battle Flag

C.S.A. Second National

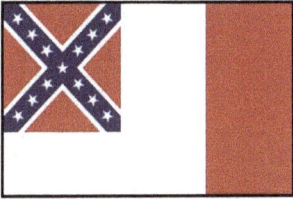

C.S.A. Third National

Scotland

Georgia (replaced)

Mississippi (replaced)

Florida

Alabama

British Union

Ireland

Nova Scotia

Jamaica

Faroe Islands

Finland

Northern Ireland

England

Iceland

Guernsey

Greece

Norway

Switzerland

Sweden

Why the South fought . . .

SEA RAVEN PRESS

THE WORLD'S #1 SOUTH-FRIENDLY BOOK PUBLISHER

Restoring Dixie's honor
Defending traditional Southern culture
Preserving authentic Confederate history
One book at a time!

Nashville, Tennessee
SeaRavenPress.com

WHAT THE
CONFEDERATE FLAG
MEANS TO ME

Americans Speak Out in Defense of
Southern Honor, Heritage, & History

I. AL BENSON JR.

Louisiana

The Confederate Flag means different things to different people, some of whom have never been taught real history.

The Confederate Flag, with its St. Andrews Cross is, to me, first and foremost, a Christian symbol. Many claim this is not so, but the St. Andrews Cross on that flag is a Christian symbol. Rather than debate that fact with us they respond by trying to label us all as "racists" which is so typical of the leftist method of operation.

Secondly, the Confederate Flag represents, to me, a symbol of resistance to tyranny. When those countries in Eastern Europe that had been part of the Soviet Empire started to break away, or secede, there were street demonstrations in those countries where Confederate flags appeared. That happened in several different countries. I saw many of the pictures of them in several different places. At least some in those countries seemed to understand that the Confederate Flag was a symbol of resistance to tyranny—something many in this country have yet to grasp—thanks to our court "historians."

I have always viewed the Confederate Flag as both a Christian symbol and a symbol of resistance to tyranny. The two views do not disagree with one another—in fact, they complement one another.

Its detractors claim the flag is "racist," yet not only white Southerners fought under its banner but also black Southerners, Native American Southerners and Hispanic Southerners. In my opinion the real racists are those who spend their time and effort trying to denigrate a flag that was, in truth, a soldiers flag for all the above-mentioned races.

I have a Confederate ancestor from North Carolina who fought under that flag. When they attack it they are attacking not only my ancestor but me and my descendants as well. When they attack that flag they are trying to destroy part of the heritage that has been bequeathed to me and my descendants and I do not take that lightly.

The north face of the Confederate Monument at Columbia, South Carolina. Created by famed sculptor Carlo Nicoli and erected in 1879 "by the women of South Carolina," the text engraved on its sides can only hint at the patriotic and emotional depths that lie behind the South's intense affection for the Confederate Flag.

Inscription on north face: "This monument perpetuates the memory of those who, true to the instincts of their birth, faithful to the teachings of their fathers, constant in their love for the State, died in the performance of their duty: Who have glorified a fallen cause by the simple manhood of their lives, the patient endurance of suffering, and the heroism of death, and who, in the dark hours of imprisonment, in the hopelessness of the hospital, in the short, sharp agony of the field, found support and consolation in the belief that at home they would not be forgotten."

Inscription on south face: "Let the stranger, who may in future times read this inscription, recognize that these were men whom power could not corrupt, whom death could not terrify, whom defeat could not dishonor, and let their virtues plead for just judgement of the cause in which they perished. Let the South Carolinian of another generation remember that the State taught them how to live and how to die. And that from her broken fortunes she has preserved for her children the priceless treasures of her memories, teaching all who may claim the same birthright that truth, courage and patriotism endure forever." — William Henry Trescot

2. BIRCH BRICKER

Newcastle, California

I've grown up and currently live in a town in the foothills of Northern California and was raised to believe in the usual myth regarding the Civil War: that it was a clear-cut fight between good guys versus bad guys. I thought I knew the story well enough; then I saw Mr. HK Edgerton on YouTube and what he had to say piqued my interest in the subject. Thus began a search to see if what he had to say was true. After reading some of Mr. Lochlainn Seabrook's works (Sea Raven Press) and a few other historians, I've come to appreciate the story in a whole new way.

The Civil War wasn't a simple case of slavery. That is intellectually dishonest and a lazy answer. War is about money and power, not morality. In a larger context the struggle was between the Jeffersonians and the Hamiltonians, or the Anti-Federalists and the Federalists. Everyone wanted slavery to end but there was disagreement on how to end it.

I live in a state that is a well known "Nanny-State." Last year California enacted 1,200 new laws. Living under such a regime has made me neither liberal nor conservative but rather a governmental minimalist. The best government is that which governs least.

When the governor of California made the wearing of masks (Corona Virus) mandatory, I initially refused. Asking me to wear one is one thing, making me is another. This caused me to think of the Civil War and the Confederate Flag. I decided that if I'm going to be made to wear a mask I would wear a Confederate Flag mask in protest. I don't mind doing something but I need to do it on my own terms. I have to admit that I was prepared for a possible confrontation the first several times I went into a store. Interestingly, I've had zero complaints but many compliments. People seem to generally like that I'm wearing a Confederate Flag and are very supportive of it. Everyone mentions how ridiculous it is to think that it's somehow racist in any way. Everyone that has spoken to me seems to understand why I'm wearing it. The only question I get is if I've had any problems. I have not.

I would personally never wear or support anything I felt was racist in any way. People of this country need an honest discussion of race, not media sound bites and the scapegoating of a symbol that they misunderstand. I feel that I am on solid ground and I support people of all color while wearing the Confederate Flag in public. I agree with the Reverend Martin Luther King when he famously said that a man ought not be judged by the color of his skin but by the content of his character. Amen.

Therefore, as a native Californian, I proudly wear the Confederate Flag as a symbol of my protest against government over-reach. To me it has become a symbol of hope. To hope that someday Californians will realize that the government here is causing most of our problems, not solving them. The Confederacy was right to struggle against what could be called Northern totalitarianism and an intrusion of local affairs. When I say the Confederacy was "right to struggle" I do not mean any kind of defense of slavery. Slavery is an institution that ultimately hurts everyone, black, white and otherwise. The Confederate soldiers died bravely, not for slavery, but for the right of self-determination. The Confederacy may have lost the battle, but the war is yet unfinished.

Conservative Kentuckian (later a Mississippian) and Confederate President Jefferson Davis: immortal Southern hero. Like the vast majority of Southerners, initially Davis did not approve of secession, and resisted it—until Liberal Lincoln and the Leftist North left Dixie no choice. Despite a few serious oversights (such as not putting Nathan Bedford Forrest in charge of the Army of Tennessee), Davis—who was loved and supported by the Southern people—performed admirably as the Confederacy's first chief executive, and would have almost certainly led the C.S.A. to victory had it not been for one simple fact: As a Christian Conservative, Davis followed the laws of the land, such as the Constitution and the Geneva Conventions. Like Leftists today, however, agnostic Liberal Lincoln felt free to disregard not only the Constitution and the Geneva Conventions, but standard military rules of conduct, national and international law, local and civil regulations, and above all, social customs built on Christian morality, civility, ethics, mutual respect, and human decency. Today we might simply call these combined laws "soldier code," something lacking in many of Lincoln's military orders. Its flagrant law-breaking approach gave the U.S. a huge and unfair advantage, one that ultimately helped lead to Lee's surrender. It is obvious who would have won the War had Lincoln obeyed the law: even with far less men, equipment, arms, funding, and time to organize, the C.S. was able to stay in the fight for four years. Later, in his memoirs, Union General Ulysses S. Grant himself noted that if the Confederacy had held on for just 12 more months, the U.S. would have been forced to let her go in triumph and freedom.

3. DR. B. L. REID

Westmoreland, Tennessee, Confederate States of America

The Confederate States Army Battleflag, represents my ancestors, who fought to defend their homes and families from an invading horde, who took what they wanted, destroyed what they could not take and burned what they felt could still be used by the citizens of our country, the South.

This legacy is what the United States Army left in our country, the South. The wanton disregard for the rules of civilized warfare. If acted on today, they would be guilty of war crimes beyond our belief. They are as guilty today, as then, and just as bad, if not worse than the Nazis of Germany or the militaristic Japanese of World War Two. They were tried for their crimes; may God hear our prayer as we all claim His promise; "Vengeance is Mine," saith the Lord, "I will repay!"

The Confederate Battleflag represents the men who stood and fought and died, defending our country from this horde of invading heathens, who looked for nothing more than booty, thievery, treachery, rape, murder, mayhem and the rule of might makes right. They are a shame to the history of the so called u.s.a. Nation and should be left on the trash heap of history.

We should fly the Confederate Battleflag, with a reverence

for the men who served under it, the families they fought to protect, and always remember, they were fighting for the *independence* of our country, the South. This is still the *unfulfilled* dream of all Southerners, from the despotic, demonic and heretical government of the so called u.s.a. Nation.

Our Confederate Battleflag is a symbol of hope, of charity, of liberty, for our people, who are treated as third class citizens today in the so called u.s.a. Nation.

Remember, and never, ever forget, that *liberty* is freedom, built on the foundation of sacrifice, of our fellow ancestors and warriors, who fought and bled and died for our country, the South.

May God bless the South, and may He grant us our liberty and our independence.

Waiting for His blessings and the hope of liberty, I am, sir, till then, in the Christian bonds of the Old South, very respectfully, your obedient servant, in His Service.

Confederate veterans schooled their children and grandchildren in the Truth *before* our South-loathing U.S. government had a chance to indoctrinate them against their own people and history. This is a practice that should be strictly adhered to by all traditional Southerners, Conservatives, and American patriots today. Pictured here is Confederate veteran Thomas Benjamin Amiss (and granddaughter) in his United Confederate Veterans (U.C.V.) uniform. Amiss was a member of Co. B, 6th Virginia Cavalry Regiment and 31st Georgia Infantry Regiment. Photo taken at Luray, Virginia, circa 1907.

4. BOBBY FEARS

Texas

The flag that has become known as the Confederate flag means several things. It's hard to say which meaning takes precedence but it's a mixture of regional, ancestral, and ideological pride. I learned of its prominence in family history and it was anathema to turn your back on your brave ancestors and former country. It was a point of pride to be from Texas but also a son of the South.

Learning the truth of that struggle only reinforced my love and devotion to it. I hate it to my very core when I see and hear all the negative, hateful, and flat out lies attributed to it. I could go on *ad nauseam*, but when I see that flag I'm filled with pride, honor, humility, inspiration, and a touch of rebel resilience. Especially here of late!

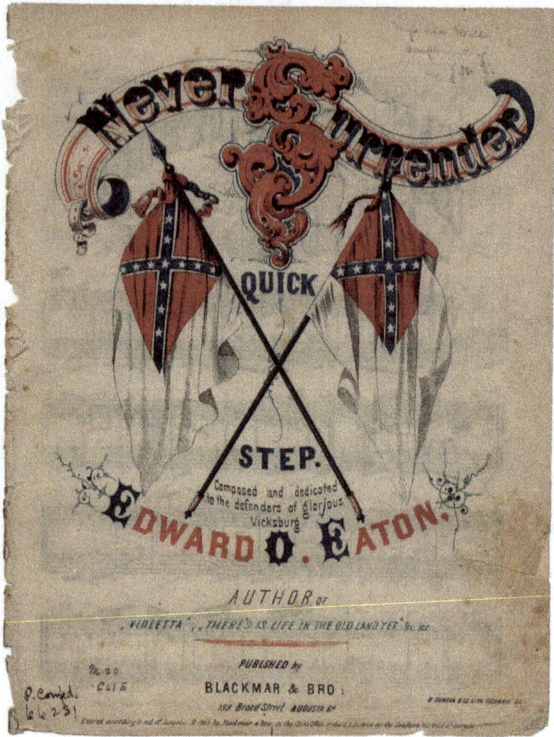

Sheet music cover of Edward O. Eaton's Confederate song, "Never Surrender Quick Step," published about 1863.

S. CHUCK JOHNSON

OWNER, RUM CREEK SUTLERY

Gray, Georgia

To me the Confederate flag is a representation of a region, a culture, a heritage, a way of life, and a society of chivalry and honor. My ancestors fought for that flag in the name of conviction and integrity. It is a source of pride that they were willing to give their lives in defense of their homes and beliefs. The Confederate flag is a symbol of that willingness.

The Southern culture has always been based in hospitality, honor, honesty, and integrity, and that flag is, to me, still a symbol of that. Being truly Southern means being true to your word, kind, welcoming, and willing to fight for what is yours and what you believe in. That has never changed.

The Confederacy was based on the same intrinsic values with which our forefathers founded the United States. A reliance upon God, morality, virtue, and respect are very important in my life and the Confederate flag is a representation, not only of my values, but of those that lived and died under it.

I am a born and bred Georgian and I take pride in that. Georgia and the South are my home, and like *all* countries and cultures, the South may have made mistakes, but we have always been a people and a heritage to be proud of the

Confederate flag, and it will always will be a symbol of that in my heart and mind.

I sincerely hope others feel that way as well.

A colorful display showing examples of some of the various flags employed by the Confederate military. Generally speaking, the square battle flag design was favored by the army while the rectangle battle flag design was favored by the navy—though the latter saw service in both military branches.

6. DOUG BOREN

Charlotte, North Carolina

Although I grew up with this flag, as a youth, I only appreciated its beauty and striking colors. It was only when I reached maturity and learned the truth of the Confederacy and their struggle for independence did I come to appreciate it so much more!

First, it represents honor. There have been no more honorable soldiers, or citizens than those of the Confederate South. The honor they embodied was the very reason for living, and to lose it would be to lose your very life.

Second, it represents resistance to tyranny. To those who believe that the war was to keep slavery, this may sound ludicrous. Those who know the truth know that was not the cause of the war. The sovereign Southern nation was invaded by a hostile and belligerent force, despite all efforts to avoid war. They simply wanted to be left alone. Homes, firesides, families and their very way of life was attacked, and the men and women of that time gave their all to defend it. The flag was a rallying symbol, an inspiration in that struggle. It still is, and not only for Southerners.

In the century or more since that illegal conflict, US soldiers flew that flag on their camps, their units, their vehicles, their tents, even on conquered battle fields, showing their proud victory. Even other countries, who have nothing to do with the Confederacy, have flown this flag as a show of independence and love of freedom. It has been seen in the Balkans, in Iraq, in Brazil, in Afghanistan, and around the globe. All meaning the same thing: resistance to tyranny.

These days, it has become a symbolic focal point to remember our heritage. It instills a sense of pride, when that feeling can be so elusive or taken away. It helps us hold our head high, and make no apologies for what we believe or who we are. It reminds us not only of our valiant ancestors, but the things in life that are good. Things like family, and an all merciful God, respect, hard work, and courage. In a world that is the antithesis to everything we believe or want, it calms us, it settles us, it is like a rock on the foundation of all things worth living for. It is like a magic looking glass that reminds us of life in simpler, happier times.

And finally, it is a symbol of hope. A hope that we as a country can return to the conservative roots that we were founded upon. *Deo Vindice!* God Vindicates!

The Confederate Flag is so significant to Southerners that they were demanding the return of C.S. flags seized during the War decades, even generations, later. This photo, taken in 1922, shows a group of men surrounding a Confederate flag that had been captured by the 118th Illinois Regiment from the 11th Tennessee Volunteers. In typical Left-wing Yankee fashion, the flag was returned to the state of Tennessee on a day important only to Northerners: April 27, the anniversary of the birth of Union General Ulysses S. Grant. Despite this affront to the South, the flag's homecoming was eagerly celebrated across the Volunteer State. Front row, left to right: Gaylord Davidson of Illinois, who made the presentation; W. C. Galloway, Commander of the Army of Northern Virginia, Confederate Veterans; Senator William B. McKinley of Illinois; Senator Kenneth McKellar of Tennessee; and Wade H. Cooper of Tennessee, representing the Governor of Tennessee in accepting the flag.

7. GARY PRICE

Rapid City, South Dakota

When I grew up in the 1960s and 1970s, most people didn't know there is a 1st, 2nd, and 3rd national flag of the old South, and a battle flag (what we commonly see is a rectangular naval jack, while the battle flag is perfectly square). I was also taught that the "stars and bars" was General Beauregard's idea and is now the state flag of Georgia, having abandoned the St Andrew's cross version representing the 11 states of the Confederacy, with honorary stars of KY and MO, who remained divided during the war.

As a direct descendant of Frank and Jesse James, I learned about injustices forced upon the old South. We were taught in TN and GA state history to revere the Confederate flag, no matter it's version, as we do the stars and stripes. If the former is about slavery, then the stars and stripes holds more guilt, as it was carried by Sherman's cavalry in the Indian wars, plus the North profited from slavery until it was no longer useful to them.

Hypocrisy is a terrible thing, and is used as propaganda to divide and conquer. It makes sure that society remains subjugated. The flag remains in the hearts and minds of those who were subjugated and hopefully, their descendants, though I have seen comments from some descendants who have changed, and not for the betterment of the flag.

Unfortunately, this symbol has been adopted by those not deserving of it, leading to a media spin who are only interested in sensationalism, lies, selling news, attracting attention and swaying voters towards their way of thinking. Politicians, as weak as they are, are only interested in their jobs, and usually do not represent the wishes of the man in the street.

Term limits might ease some of this. Mississippi has no state flag until 2021 for this reason and Georgia accepted a watered down version of the flag. Counties across America who had the flag displayed on police uniforms, cars, and buildings have also abandoned the flag. This happened recently in Gettysburg, SD, when someone from the left complained. Pandering and giving in seems to be the flavor of the era.

Some folks stand their ground, such as the manager of the Murdo Car show in SD, who holds a version of the General Lee, and when an objection came forward regarding the flag on the top of the car, was told that the General wouldn't be the General without the flag, and if the tourists in question didn't like it, they didn't have to return to see it.

We should all stand our ground this way. Ignore the media, and the no-goods who abuse and misuse the flag. Those who feel it is racist should consider the US flag, flown by Sherman's troops in the Indian wars and noted long before the Confederacy existed, when the colonies first formed a Union.

A drawing of Fort Sumter, with a tattered Confederate Second National Flag floating proudly over the ruins of the garrison.

8. GIL LUNA

Las Vegas, Nevada

I grew up in Los Angeles, CA, and was taught that the Civil War was one "between the States" but never really the reasons as to why. It wasn't until I was in my twenties that I learned that it was all about states rights—and only states rights.

Having grown up in Los Angeles, you would be amazed as to the amount of true Southerners that I came across. They were proud of their heritage, and to be honest were some of the most kind and generous people that l grew up with.

I have traveled to the southern parts of the United States, Arkansas, Oklahoma and Louisiana and have felt more comfortable there—genuinely more comfortable, than in Los Angeles, my home town.

So now to the question: what does the Confederate Flag mean to me? It means that it holds a heritage that has become almost lost here in America. It means being part of a community so long as you are accepting of it. It means that you are amongst the most godly, patriotic and family oriented society that in other parts of this great nation, are almost hidden away.

The flag does not mean hate to me and it never did. I know that there are many "snowflakes" that would beg to differ—and almost scream their hatred and ignorance of that fact.

For me the Confederate flag stands for, and has stood for traditional values and ways of thinking. It stands for a people that are willing to put it all on the line for their beliefs. It means that it is a symbol of a people who will not only talk a good talk, but back it up with actions. It is a symbol of uniting behind a cause and regardless of the odds, defending it to the end.

The Confederate flag is not a symbol of hate—it is a symbol of hope. A symbol of defending what you believe to be right and not backing down. It has been tarnished and has been bastardized by forces that do not comprehend its true meaning. If you did, it would be flown proudly next to the "Stars and Stripes." It is as meaningful to me as the American Flag, since it *is* America.

Many people will disagree with these statements, and that is OK since it is just that—their opinion. My thoughts and actions are based on facts, not only what I have learned—but also what I have seen. That is a powerful incentive and a reason to be proud of our Confederate flag.

God Bless.

The demonization of the South and her symbols is not a modern phenomenon. In this typical Left-wing, anti-South propaganda handbill from 1861, Confederate leaders (left) are portrayed as being in league with the Devil and his minions (right). On the left (from left to right) are: "Mr. Mob Law, Chief Justice" (that is, a street ruffian), General Pierre G. T. Beauregard (on horseback), Secretary of State Robert Toombs, and President Jefferson Davis and Vice President Alexander H. Stephens holding a list of "The Fundamental Principles of our Government: Treason, Rebellion, Murder, Robbery, Incendiarism, and Theft." Satan, holding a South Carolina flag, tells the Confederates that they are "truly fit representatives of our Realm." The malicious and duplicitous Left-wing Party of the 1860s (then the Republican Party, led by big government Liberal Lincoln) also falsely Satanized the white South for "racism" against blacks, fabricating tall tales about the KKK and African Americans, inventions still used to this day to defame, censor, and control the South and her people. As anyone who has read my books knows, however, what I call the "Reconstruction KKK" was a purely political (pro-Constitution) organization founded by Southern Conservatives, who were being illegally prevented from holding political office in their own states at the time. This organization—which was intentionally formed as a temporary group and thus lasted a mere three years or so—had absolutely nothing to do with race, and, contrary to modern Liberal mythology, has no connection whatsoever to today's KKK, which arose much later (in the early 20th Century). Progressives will never tell you, for example, that there was an all black KKK chapter in Nashville, one that heartily supported the Conservative agenda of the South. It was, in fact, the Left (the North, Yankees, the U.S.A.) which used blacks as political pawns before, during, and after the War, not the Right (the South, Confederates, the C.S.A.). (To learn more about the Reconstruction KKK see my book, *Nathan Bedford Forrest and the Ku Klux Klan: Yankee Myth, Confederate Fact*. Spring Hill, TN: Sea Raven Press, 2016.) Projection (reversing reality) is, of course, an established Left-wing strategy in the Information War between Right and Left, for the truth of the matter is that the Confederacy was godly (like its Christian chief executive Davis), while the Union was ungodly (like its anti-Christian chief executive Lincoln)—making a mockery of the anti-South disinformation flyer pictured here.

9. GLORIA PEOPLES-ELAM

PARKER COUNTY HISTORICAL COMMISSION MEMBER AUTHOR AND HISTORIAN

Springtown, Parker County, Texas

In a book I wrote and published in 2013 I had traced my family, the Peebles/Peoples back to 1649 in America. My ancestor Capt. David Peebles came to settle on the James River. I wrote about those beginnings in my book *An American Heritage Story: Tracing the Ancestry of William Henry Peoples and Elizabeth Washington Peoples.*

Some family members began to migrate into South Carolina where they lived (and many descendants still do) for over 100 years. The Civil War that some southerners call "The War of Northern Aggression" was a war that the Peebles/Peoples family fought for their rights. My ancestors migrated through the southern states.

At the start of the war my great great grandparents William and Elizabeth (Washington) Peoples (changed by census takers) were living in Choctaw County, Mississippi. Their first son was named George Washington Peoples. They loved their heritage and the link to our first President of the United States of America. William and his son George, as did many of the Peoples/Peebles clan, joined the Confederacy soon after the war began. Throughout the southern states there were members of the family joining the Confederacy and proud to carry the Confederate flag. Just prior to the war

William sent Elizabeth and the younger members of the family to East Texas. They were safer there than they would have been in Mississippi.

Elizabeth's brother, Jeremiah Washington and his family, were already in Texas living in Cass County. Jeremiah joined the Fourth Regiment Co. D, C.S.A. Terry's Texas Rangers. Also, J. T. Washington, son of Jeremiah was listed as being in the Thirteenth Regiment, Co. C, Infantry. In fact, two of Texas' best known fighting units were Terry's Texas Rangers (Eighth Texas Cavalry) and the infantry of Hood's Brigade. These Texas Rangers were described by a Union officer as being "quick as lightning."

The ancestral connection to men in my Peoples and Washington family has endeared me to the Confederacy. My DNA runs deep in a connection to these men and women of the southern states. My library is chock-full of the many books about the "War of Northern Aggression" better known as The Civil War. My books on George Washington are just as numerous. The Confederate flag means a lot to me, but just as the American flag does as well. The Texas flag is equally special to me. Those three flags are my identity for who I am and my heritage.

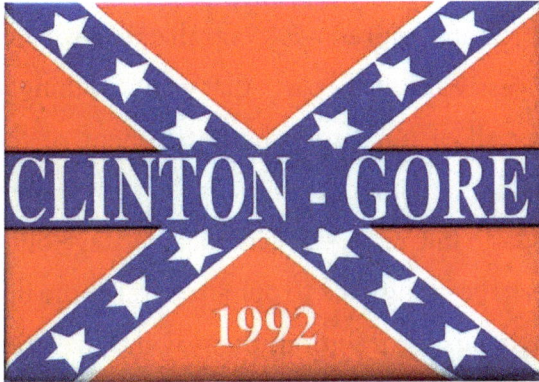

In 1992 the Democratic Party (or someone associated with it) put the Clinton-Gore campaign logo on a Confederate Battle Flag badge. No one denounced it or tried to have it banned. Neither Bill Clinton or Al Gore, both Liberals, were called "racists." Why? Because it was not yet advantageous for the Left to fully demonize the Confederate Flag. Although the U.S. government was issuing anti-Confederate Flag statutes as far back as Reconstruction (1865-1877), it would not be until the 21st Century that sociopolitical events induced Liberals to begin routinely using the Starry Cross as a weapon against the Conservative South. On October 13, 2016, Conservative U.S. President Donald J. Trump said: "There is nothing the political establishment will not do, and no lie they will not tell, to hold onto their prestige and power at your expense. The Washington establishment, and the financial and media corporations that fund it, exists for only one reason: to protect and enrich itself." These are the same sentiments voiced by Conservative Southerners in the 1850s and 1860s.

10. JAMES JOHNSON

Florida

The Confederate flag to me means the courage to stand up to an oppressive centralized government and oppressive political party that wants nothing more than power over all of our lives, the enrichment of their crony friends, and the impoverishment of all Americans. It represents faith in Christ, the Christian heritage of my family, and our heritage going back to our ancestral home in Scotland. I believe it stands for tradition, the way that we grew up, not changing for the sake of change.

The flag represents a chance to live without fear of government telling you how much water to flush, what to believe, or to wear a mask that doesn't stop viruses just to be part of the crowd. It represents history, the struggle of a people to continue to live the way they've chosen to live, who believed that theirs was the same struggle as those in the American Revolution, protecting their right to self-government from those who wanted to place all power in a distant capital that wasn't accountable to the people who put them there. And with that, it represents a sadness at the needless suffering and trauma the South suffered at the hands of a people who believed that anyone who disagreed with them were evil and needed to be destroyed, much like one of the modern political parties, and had no right to try to escape their desire to control them and suck money from them.

I cry when I think of the suffering of people burned out of their houses, losing every possession, losing their sons, and their daughter's "innocence" at the hands of a people filled with a false righteousness of their cause of omnipotent Nationalist government that dictates every aspect of our lives, the true definition of fascism, cloaked in false morality (virtue-signaling) to assuage their consciences rather than just letting them go in peace.

I don't see it as a flag of racism or slavery, as thousands of Confederates fought under the flag to defend their homes from invasion, including thousands of blacks, Hispanics, and Asians, voluntarily. Lee hated slavery, Jackson ran a black Sunday School, Davis adopted a black boy, while Lincoln wanted to deport emancipated blacks out of the country at war's end. The American flag was just as misused by racists, but that doesn't mean the American flag is inherently racist.

Finally, to me the Confederate flag represents the future hope of freedom from tyranny for all Americans of all races, to remind them all that we can stand up to an oppressive central government, together as one people, without regard to race, and say "No!" to the technocrats who think their fifteen Ivy League degrees and no real-life experience mean they know better how to run everyone's lives without having to live by the same rules they set for us. I see it flying when traveling and it gives me hope that one day, we might be as free as our ancestors once were.

This worn and faded 158 year old drawing, created by artist Alfred R. Waud in 1863, depicts the Battle of Gettysburg, July 1-3, 1863. A Confederate color bearer, on the left, is struggling valiantly to hold the Battle Flag aloft as Union forces (right) pour a galling fire of lead into the advancing Southern lines.

II. JAMES PIERCE

Franklinton, North Carolina

It's become popular today to call the flag a symbol of hate and slavery. The flag has been used by some fringe groups to promote their brand of hatred. History is in the process of being rewritten in order to support that narrative. To add to that narrative it's been suggested that Confederates of all ranks and Southerners in general are traitors: the South for leaving the Union and the commanders for resigning the Union army and joining the Confederacy.

The flag represents the army that formed to resist the promised Union invasion by the federal government whose power is granted by the states. That separation of powers was the cause for which they fought and the flag the rally point.

If you are assured that your home was to be invaded and the invaders will press upon you and your family, you have but two choices. Bow to that will or stand and fight. They chose to fight. That's what that battle flag means.

As this photo demonstrates, in 1962 the Confederate Battle Flag was a common and accepted sight at universities and college sports events across the South. Some 60 years later it has all but disappeared. What changed? Socialists and communists began smearing the flag with the "racist" epithet. But calling something or someone racist does not make it so, anymore than saying Monday is Tuesday or red is blue. Gaslighting causes a lie to *appear* true, however, which is why this villainous technique is a favorite tool of the Left.

12. JASON PRATHER

Lincoln, Nebraska

I am ashamed to say growing up the Confederate Flag was a symbol of hatred and racism, but when I started to study on my own from the actual Southerner's writings that were not destroyed by the Northern occupation of the South, she became a thing of beauty, honor, strength and loyalty. I began to appreciate her more and more and have no problem seeing her flying and am willing to defend her from any if not all opposition if possible.

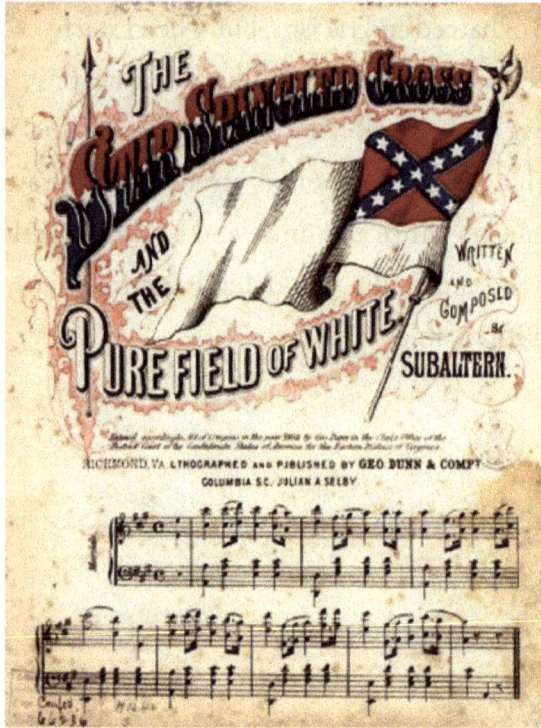

Sheet music cover of the Victorian Confederate song, "The Star Spangled Cross and the Pure Field of White."

13. J. SANFORD KRUIZENGA

Tennessee (Michigan transplant)

Though the Confederate Battle Flag was a military banner representing the brave Southern people of multiple races who fought, bled, and/or died against oppressive Northern invaders hell-bent on reconstructing the South in its own image, today when I view the flag I see it as the ultimate symbol of freedom from oppressive authority as it bears the Cross of St. Andrew, the same cross the Scots fought under in seeking freedom from the English tyrants.

Confederate monument with Confederate Battle Flags and cannon, Livingston, Alabama, circa 1915. Thanks to their enlightened patriotic mothers and fathers, these early 20th-Century youngsters grew up with a positive wholesome view of the Confederacy, their Confederate ancestors, and the Southern Cause.

14. KEVIN J. MILLER

DIRECTOR CAMP MOORE CONFEDERATE MUSEUM & CEMETERY
Tangipahoa, Louisiana

The Confederate Flag to me represents those gallant and patriotic people who stood for the right and in memory of all those that fought for, sacrificed for, believed in, and gave their lives to establish this country originally.

The Confederate Flag not only represents those peoples of old, but also their unwavering belief that a people should have the right to govern themselves without an oppressive government imposing their will, their control, and in fact their totalitarian rule over anyone.

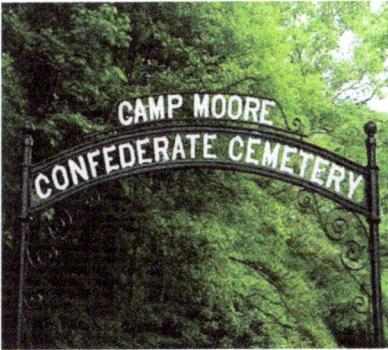

As I look at the Confederate Flag today, I am filled with pride in those that fought under it, to attempt to break away from a government that has lost sight of our original Founders' ideals for this great country, and what it would become. One Nation of States bound for the common good of all, under the understanding that it is a voluntary Confederacy, of the same, with respect for each state to govern their own people without intervention or dictatorship of any other state or a large government bent on imposing its will over the citizens of the voluntary member states.

God would it be, that those that are opposed to, or offended by the Flag of the Confederacy, would with the same zeal, do the historical research necessary to understand just what it stands for, why so many fought under it, supported it, and revered it, and what this flag means to those of us that fly it.

Any fool can object to anything when they are uninformed or a social lemming, but a wise person researches and considers historical fact, not socially engineered teaching or spoon feeding.

A Victorian artist's rendering of the Confederacy's Second National Flag, surrounded by various notable battle scenes. A Confederate Battle Flag shield and damaged field cannon (at bottom center) serve as symbols of the heroic Confederate dead.

15. KIMBERLY PARKER

Tennessee

To me the Confederate Flag is a memorial to the soldiers who fought in the war, and it's also a symbol of Southern ancestry.

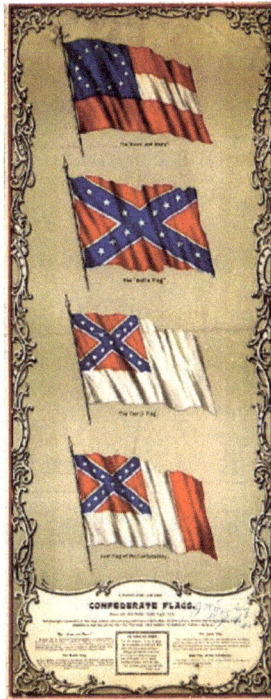

A Confederate "Civil War" souvenir card with illustrations of the Confederacy's four official flags. Top to bottom: 1) First National, the "Stars and Bars"; 2) Battle Flag, the "Southern Cross"; 3) Second National, the "Stainless Banner"; 4) Third National, the "Blood Stained Banner"—the last and still current official national flag of the Confederate States of America. The C.S. First National Flag, the Stars and Bars, was never demonized by the Left and so is not falsely associated with racism, hate, slavery, or treason. Thus many 21st-Century Confederates display it instead of the other three C.S.A. flags. The seven star version of the First National is the official logo (and flag) of the United Daughters of the Confederacy. While the designer of the Battle Flag, William Porcher Miles, is well-known, the designer of the First National Flag is still debated: in the early 1900s both Nicola Marschall (from Prussia) and Orren Randolph Smith (from North Carolina) claimed to be the original artist.

16. KURT SCHLUCHTER

Woodstock, Georgia

What does the Confederate flag mean to me? My American heritage is mixed between Northern and Southern, all my family immigrated here before the 1860s. I had family on both sides of the Civil War.

The Confederate battle flag ultimately is the symbol of Southern heritage and resistance to tyranny and oppression, "it isn't racial what-so-ever; it's Southern." Those who see it racially in my mind are the so-called racists who hate the South and Christian conservatives, and are guilty of obfuscation and slander willfully or ignorantly.

To understand the battle flag, you have to study immigration patterns in the 18th and 19th centuries. The South had a huge influx of Scots-Irish immigrants. These pioneering immigrants who came to this country fleeing poverty and persecution from Britain had no interest in the over-zealous puritanical North; "it reminded them of the land they fled," and they ventured south to Appalachia pursuing their yeoman way of life.

The X on the flag represents the Christian Cross of St. Andrew the first disciple of Christ, brother to Simon Peter, the same X shown on the Scottish Flag for the same reason. St. Andrew was crucified because he refused to stop preaching the gospel of Christ in Greece where they still believed and worshiped the Roman gods, and he was crucified on an X rather than a cross. He said he was not worthy to be crucified on a cross like Jesus.

When the war broke out in 1861 the fighting spirit of these men immediately rallied to the revolutionary cause of independence, as they felt resistance to the tyranny in their blood based on 100s of years of persecution. The very motto of the Confederate States, *Deo Vindice*, is the spirit of their cause and of that battle flag which means "under God as our vindicator." When I hear popular culture seeking to slander that flag, I see the Devil himself, "known as the great accuser," at work. Across the world throughout the last 161 years that flag has served as the rallying flag against tyranny and oppression. When I look at the battle flag, I see a military Christian symbol representing standing up to oppression and tyranny under great odds.

Those who slander this Southern symbol do so from a place of hate for Christianity and racial intolerance. Those who denigrate that symbol from a place of racial hate do so without permission from the sons and daughters of the Confederacy. I hear the excuse that it was used by the KKK often; but those who understand the difference between the 19th century Southern KKK, "that was disbanded after Reconstruction," and the 20th century "deep state" KKK understand that the 20th century KKK was not Southern, but a deep state entity used for propaganda. This 20th century deep state KKK also used the Christian Bible, cross, and the American flag as a symbol of white supremacy, so that argument is null.

I am happy to have my comments recorded under my name. I've already been persecuted for my beliefs many times and am not scared to stand up for them. It's an honor.

The Confederate Battle Flag was once welcomed in Southern churches. This watercolor, for example, is a design drawing of a stained glass window intended for Saint James Episcopal Church, Richmond, Virginia. It portrays Sally Louisa Tompkins, who founded and operated Robertson Hospital soon after the start of Lincoln's War, where she and her staff cared for the Confederate wounded from July 1861 to June 1865. At the top of the drawing is a scene of the hospital with a Confederate Battle Flag flying over the entrance. Confederate President Jefferson Davis recognized the value of Tompkins' service and delegated her a Confederate captain on September 9, 1861—making her the first woman commissioned by the C.S.A. While she cared for over 1,300 soldiers at her private hospital for four years, Captain Tompkins refused the salary offered her by the Confederate army, insisting that it instead go toward the treatment of her patients. An active member of Saint James Episcopal Church, she was known as "the angel of the Confederacy," and several chapters of the United Daughters of the Confederacy have been named after her. Captain Tompkins passed away in 1916 and was buried with full military honors. Were this notable Confederate humanitarian alive today, she would not be happy with the deceitful Left's blasphemous treatment of the Confederate Flag.

17. LOCHLAINN SEABROOK

CREATOR & EDITOR OF THIS BOOK

Nashville, Tennessee

As an author-scholar of over 50 "Civil War" related books, I have a quadruple perspective on the Confederate Battle Flag, viewing it as: 1) a Southerner, 2) a Christian, 3) a Conservative, and 4) a historian.

1) I am a 7th generation Kentuckian and a 17th generation Southerner with ancestors not only from the Bluegrass State, but also from Virginia, West Virginia, North Carolina, and Tennessee. I have hundreds of close cousins, thousands of distant cousins, and numerous ancestors who fought for and supported the Confederacy.

In the latter category were my 3rd great-grandparents: Confederate Private Elias Jent Sr. (1st Regiment, 13th Kentucky Cavalry, known as "Caudill's Army") and his wife Rachel Cornett, both who were hanged at gunpoint by Yankees while he was on furlough in 1864—just one of the countless heinous war crimes committed by Left-wing Yankees (with Lincoln's tacit approval) against my people.[17]

Additionally, while I am cousins with Robert E. Lee, Nathan Bedford Forrest, Stonewall Jackson, and Jefferson Davis, I am a direct descendant of the ancestors of Alexander

---

17. For more on this story see my book, *A Rebel Born: A Defense of Nathan Bedford Forrest.* 2010. Franklin, TN: Sea Raven Press, 2011 ed.

H. Stephens, John Singleton Mosby, William Giles Harding, and Edmund Winchester Rucker, strong Confederates all. I love and display the Confederate Battle Flag in honor of the names and memories of these, my stalwart and fearless Southern kinfolk who gave all for the right of self-government.

2) The diagonal cross on the Confederate Battle Flag is not merely a random graphic design casually placed on the banner as an eye-catching artistic element. It is the Christian Cross. To be more precise, it is one of many versions of the Christian Cross, in this case one known as the Flag of Saint Andrew, borrowed—according to William G. Swan (a Confederate veteran, a Tennessee state representative in the Confederate Congress, and a mayor of Knoxville, Tennessee)—from Scotland's national flag.

The use of the X-shaped cross in the Confederate Battle Flag can be traced back to Andrew's unusual crucifixion. According to ancient Christian legend, around 60 A.D. the humble saint, believing it would be inappropriate for him to be hung on the same type of T-shaped cross as Jesus, requested that the Romans substitute it with an X-shaped cross, or saltire, as it is properly known. Scottish legend states that nearly thirteen hundred years later, in 1314—after a series of supernatural events connected to the Scottish army and Andrew—he was named the patron saint of Scotland. Subsequently, in 1385, his diagonal cross, also known as the crux decussata ("intersecting cross"), was adopted as the country's official national flag.

When it came time for the Confederate government to design a military flag suited for the battlefield, its members, being mainly Christians of European heritage, chose Saint Andrew's Cross. The bright white saltire had a myriad of advantages, including high visibility on the field of action, an aesthetically pleasing design on which to place the stars of the seceded Southern states, and above all overt Christian symbolism. I love and display the Confederate Battle Flag in honor of my Lord and Savior and the eponymous religion that preserves his teachings on "the Gospel of the Kingdom of God" (Mark 1:14) and "the kingdom within" (Luke 17:21).[18]

3) My Confederate ancestors were Democrats, the Conservative party in the 1860s, led by Southern Conservative Democrat Jefferson Davis. Like the majority of Conservatives today, Victorian Confederates believed in small limited government, states' rights, constitutional principles, patriotism, individualism, and the core values of traditional Western culture and Christianity—in a word, Americanism.

The U.S. government at that time was Republican, the Left-wing party in the 1860s, led by Northern Liberal Republican Abraham Lincoln, whose administration and armies he packed with socialists and communists, many who were foreigners. These included, among many others that could be named, hardened anti-American radicals and anti-

---

18. For more on these important scriptural topics see my book, *Seabrook's Bible Dictionary of Traditional and Mystical Christian Doctrines*. Spring Hill, TN: Sea Raven Press, 2016.

capitalist revolutionaries like Charles Dana, August Willich, Robert Rosa, Fritz Anneke, Max Weber, and Carl Schurz.

At that time the progressive Union, like the Left today, believed in a large unlimited national government, the destruction of states' rights, a weak constitution (or none at all), agnosticism and atheism, multiculturalism (in name only), submission by the individual to the federal government, and the ascent to ultimate power and control "by any means necessary"—including social, political, and economic warfare, subterfuge, and domestic terrorism. (Note: The Democrats and the Republicans would not become the organizations we know today until the presidential election of 1896, when the two parties switched platforms, the former becoming Left-wing, the latter becoming Right-wing.)[19]

The conservative-leaning Founding Fathers created the United States of America as what they called a "Confederate Republic," named our country's first constitution "The Articles of Confederation," gave her the term of endearment "the Confederacy," and nicknamed her "The Confederate States of America"—the exact name used in 1861 by my Southern Confederate ancestors for their own new republic.[20] I love and display the Confederate Flag because I am a Conservative.

4) As a Conservative Southern historian, when it comes to

---

19. For an in-depth discussion of this topic see my book, *Abraham Lincoln Was a Liberal, Jefferson Davis Was a Conservative: The Missing Key to Understanding the American Civil War*. Spring Hill, TN: Sea Raven Press, 2017.

20. For more on these topics see my book, *Confederacy 101: Amazing Facts You Never Knew About America's Oldest Political Tradition*. Spring Hill, TN: Sea Raven Press, 2015.

the War Between the States—the War for Southern Independence, as we like to call it here in Tennessee—I own, study, read, and research historic writings by *both* Southern/Confederate authors *and* Northern/Union authors. This is quite unlike most pro-North Left-wing historians, who, because they cannot abide cognitive dissonance (the psychological discomfort that results from learning facts that challenge one's personal beliefs), are highly prone to confirmation bias (the habit of only looking at information that supports one's current beliefs). Thus they tend to read books only by other pro-North, pro-Lincoln, anti-South writers. This makes my research methodology among the majority of historians quite unique.

Because of this my perspective on the Southern Confederacy is also unique: over many decades, and with a personal library of some 30,000 books, I have read and studied both sides in the greatest detail, weighing the words of the South and the North carefully and objectively. My conclusion was, and still is, that the South was entirely correct in seceding from the Union, for religious, moral, ethical, political, social, cultural, and economic reasons too numerous to mention here. I love and display the Confederate Flag because I know the Truth about American history and "the War of the Constitution," as General Lee correctly referred to it.

Union General August Willich, one of the many communists in the U.S. army. The Prussian born revolutionary was a "Forty-Eighter" who fought in the failed European socialist revolt in 1848. Fleeing to America, he supported Lincoln and the then Left-wing Republican Party. The "ardent communist" and follower of Karl Marx recruited some 1,500 Germans into the U.S. army—many of them socialists and fellow communists.

At a Confederate Veterans Reunion circa 1917, two former Confederate soldiers from Georgia proudly display the bullet-riddled Confederate Battle Flag they carried into battle in the war against the tyranny of the Liberal North.

18. MICHAEL & JULIA DAVIS

Dixie Outfitters, Lynchburg, Tennessee

The Battle Flag is in my DNA. It means family and the ultimate act of defiance against tyranny. This is the flag of our ancestors for me and my wife. Proud members of the SCV and UDC.

My flag does not come down. Learn the true history and you will not be offended.

Deo Vindice! (God Will Vindicate)

The old Mississippi State Flag and a Confederate Battle Flag float in the wind in an unidentified yard—a scene that should warm the heart of every American patriot. This is not just a sign that the owner loves Dixie and is proud of his or her Southern heritage. Contrary to the fake history fabricated by the Left (and foolishly perpetuated by many uneducated Conservatives), the Confederate Battle Flag is a symbol of the Southern Cause: Americanism; that is, American traditions and ideals, including patriotism, states' rights, and constitutionalism.

19. PATRICK W. MERRITT

Huffman, Texas

The Confederate Battle Flag represents the honor and struggle that was the South during the Civil War. The Flag is a very important symbol of the hardships faced by our ancestors and the honor of all the men that fought, from the lowest private to some of the truly great men that came together to make the United States what it was before the recent election.

It is hard for us to understand the honor code of our ancestors in the 2021 world of dishonest and corrupt leadership. This was a time when men lined up under this flag, walked into gunfire, and died in lines because of these principles and convictions.

I hope I am not part of the generation that fails to continue to recognize the symbol of the sacrifices of these men. I believe it should be enough for everyone to be proud of the hardships their ancestors suffered to bring life to each of their families. Hopefully all of this history will not be erased.

After giving thought and study to what slavery actually was, I cannot imagine anyone ever believing this was acceptable. I am proud of the United States for spending the last 150 years working toward a better union. That does nothing to lessen the pride I have in the fact that my great-great-grandfather suffered the hardships of this war fighting under this symbol from '61 through '64 where he had a leg shot off fighting with Cleburne at Franklin and then made it all the way back to Arkansas to start the family that became us.

Confederate veteran Private Clark Robertson Starnes of Co. C, 1st North Carolina Cavalry Regiment, posing with his Confederate medals and several Confederate flags, circa 1910. Essentially, by embracing and teaching the Left's fake "Civil War" history, the U.S. government has sided with communism—ultimately, the very thing the Southern people took up arms to prevent.

20. PERCIVAL BEACROFT

TRUSTEE OF THE JEFFERSON DAVIS PAPERS
Woodville, Mississippi

I was asked my feelings toward the Confederate battle flag. My first answer is one of heritage. Most of us Southerners have blood from the British Isles. The Confederate battle flag is taken from the beautiful Scottish Cross of Saint Andrew. The Scots fought for their freedom from England just as the South was fighting for its freedom from the Northern invaders.

However, a more personal meaning to me is due to my ancestors having fought a most courageous war against the Northern armies. They fought an enemy with five times the manpower, with no treasury, no army, no navy—and a yet to be organized government—for four long years and nearly won!

This flag represents their courage, their resolve to defend their homes and families, and defend their rights as guaranteed under the federal Constitution—which was being denied them. Jefferson Davis would never never give up, and when a pardon was offered him he refused it, stating that accepting it would be admitting he had committed a wrongdoing.

All that is what the battle flag means to me.

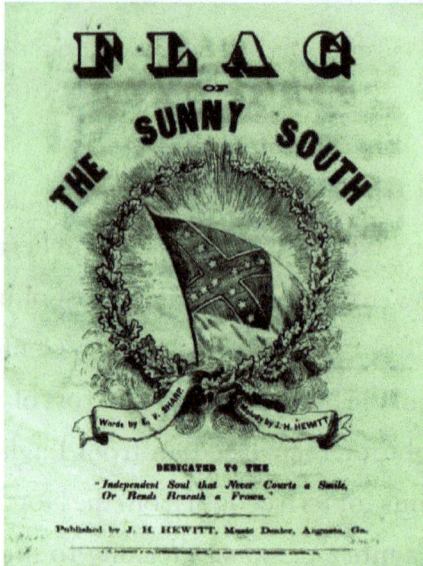

Sheet music cover of the Confederate song, "Flag of the Sunny South," by E. V. Sharp and J. H. Hewitt.

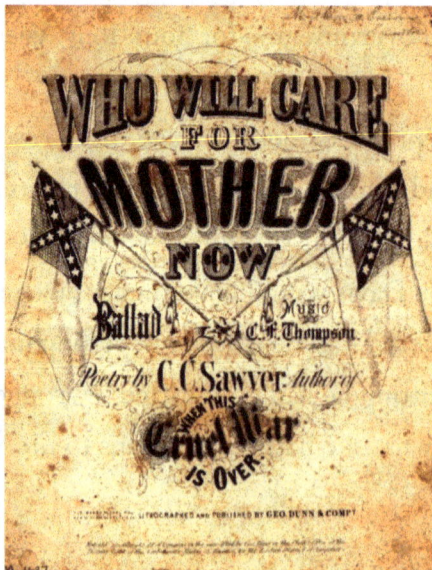

Cover of the Victorian sheet music for the Confederate song, "Who Will Care for Mother Now," by C. F. Thompson and C. C. Sawyer.

21. ROBERT ALLEN

Franklin, Tennessee

As a person raised in the Land of Lincoln by parents from Kentucky and Tennessee, Southern culture was presented to me frequently. The warmth and civility of my parents and grandparents created a deep love and devotion in return. Of course I was aware of the Civil War, although I do not remember any discussions about it within the family.

There was not a Confederate Flag hanging on a wall or flying on a pickup truck. In fact I am not certain what side any distant relatives supported or fought for.

Later in life I found my work assignment was going to be in Louisville, traveling throughout Kentucky and Tennessee. There was a distinct feeling within me of being at home, locating places and relatives I may have heard of but never personally knew. In particular were some of the brothers and sisters in Eastern Tennessee of my grandfather. He was killed at the very end of WWI, one month before my father was born.

So why am I taking your time to tell you things? Simply to voice a bit of my history and express my love for the "Southern" way of life and family.

This leads me to the "Confederate Flag" and what it means to me. To me today and on December 20, 1860, the flag represents "Southern" heritage and pride, not slavery and racism. That is a completely different discussion. Yet slavery is most often said to be the primary cause of the Civil War along with oppressive economic mandates from the South's viewpoint.

To me 260,000 Southern men and boys did not leave their loved ones behind to fight for slavery. The vast majority of the Confederate troops did not own a plantation or slaves. They went to war to recapture their liberty and maintain their culture and future. That is what I think when I see the Confederate Flag.

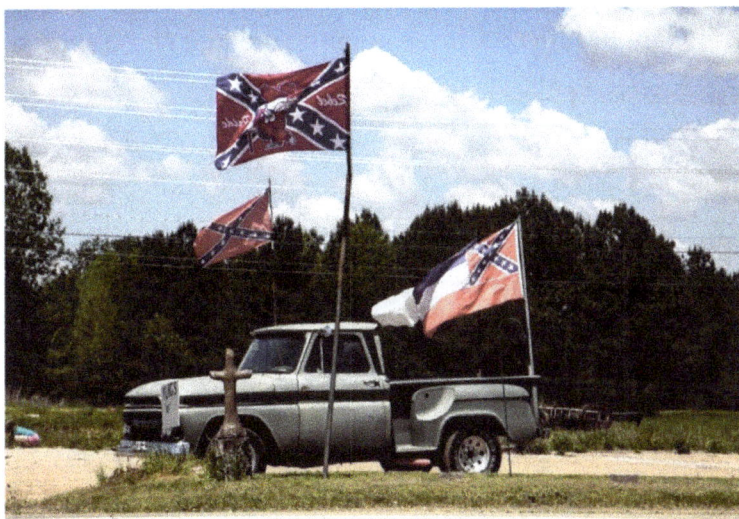

To us here in Dixie the Confederate Battle Flag is as sacred as the U.S. National Flag is to Yankees, and we will display it wherever, however, and whenever we can.

22. ROBERT CASTELLO

OWNER, DIXIE GENERAL STORE
Heflin, Alabama

I see Southern culture when viewing the Confederate flag. I think of the hundreds of thousands of people sacrificing so much to preserve our special way of life, one based on strong families, deep Christian faith, and a sincere reverence for the special culture developed by our ancestors.

My great-great-grandfather joined the Confederate army at the age of 46 to fight under the flag. I think of him, my family in the past up to the present, who loved the South and sacrificed so much for the special place in the heart of Dixie we call home.

The Confederate flag is the prime example of faith, family, service, sacrifice, and heritage. It should not be seen a symbol of division between the Southern and Northern states. I feel very proud to celebrate our flag, and I'm honor bound to continue to celebrate it.

An African American man in military garb, circa 1913. Though little is known about this photo, the individual appears to be a Civil War veteran, and most likely a Confederate soldier, since he is posing with a Confederate Battle Flag. (Union soldiers did not normally take photographs with Confederate paraphernalia unless the items had been captured in battle, and this flag clearly did not experience warfare.) Two small flags are pinned to the gentleman's jacket: a U.S. Flag and a C.S. Third National Flag—perhaps a gesture of postwar sectional unity. Yankees illegally burned down many of the South's courthouses during the War, then later dishonestly claimed "there are no records of African American Confederate soldiers, therefore it is a myth." Fortunately, the reality of the black Confederate was well chronicled, and thus many of these documents survived the War. We have "proof of service" papers, conscription, enlistment, and enrollment records, official Confederate military communications, pension applications (by widows and by the soldiers themselves), approved pensions, reception of pension checks, names on muster rolls and military rosters, prisoner of war records, exemption records, personal servant lists, discharge records, hospital records, death and cemetery records, written personal accounts (from both Confederate soldiers and Union soldiers), Confederate veteran reunion records, and above all photographs (see, for example, page 108 of this book). The final proof: on March 13, 1865, the C.S.A. government itself authorized the enrollment of blacks. Though too late to have any impact on the outcome of the War, numerous blacks entered Confederate service in the final weeks, joining forces with the hundreds of thousands of African American Confederates already serving—most in unofficial capacities, and therefore not recorded.

23. ROBERT M. SCHWARTZ

Houston, Texas

The Confederate Battle Flag is not racist nor a rebel flag. The Scots-Irish brought Scotland's nation flag with them. It is a religious flag with Andrew's (Apostle) cross on it.

The battle flag is a symbol of Christian faith and our heritage. The red field indicates nautical prowess, boldness, courage, and valor. The white indicates purity, innocence, and gentleness. The blue indicates justice, faith, perseverance, and vigilance.

The stars represent the 11 Confederate States plus 2 unseceded state governments in exile (Kentucky and Missouri). The stars (3 on each arm) represent the 12 tribes of Israel and the center star represents the priestly tribe of Levi. My family fought under this flag.

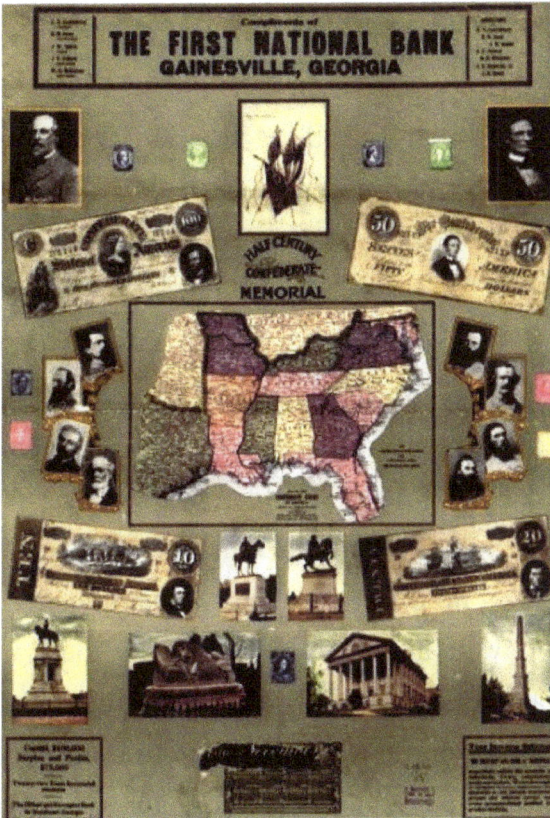

Before the recent complete vilification of Dixie took place (during the global communist uprising of 2020), Southern businesses regularly and voluntarily honored the Confederacy publicly. This early 20th-Century sign from the First National Bank of Gainesville, Georgia, for example, pays tribute to Confederate leaders, officers, soldiers, flags, buildings, statues, monuments, currency, and even Confederate postage stamps.

24. SANDRA GRIFFITH FISH

CHAPTER HISTORIAN & TREASURER CONFEDERATE RIDERS OF AMERICA

Cumberland County, Tennessee

What does the Confederate Battle Flag mean to me? I stand in the little Methodist Church cemetery in Grassy Cove, Tennessee, and look over the graves of 7 Confederate soldiers. I wish I could personally talk to them and ask them to tell me the stories of what they experienced, the good and the bad. I placed Confederate battle flags at each grave marker, lest they be forgotten.

I look to my right and see 3 family member soldiers buried together. Did they fight shoulder to shoulder? Were they wounded or killed in battle? The bravery it took to stand together with millions of others to fight to defend their southern way of life, their rights denied them under the Constitution of the United States, and for their families.

So much dread and terror it was to bear for their fathers, mothers, wives and children as to the unknown state of return. The guts and determination they had to march to a possible impeding, but dedication to duty, death to uphold the belief in the freedom from a Union that expected much and gave so little. The pride they felt fighting under that great beautiful flag that flew tattered, torn and bloody as a beacon of hope, courage and love for their Southern home soil. It resulted in making boys into men and all into heroes.

What does the Confederate Battle Flag mean to me? It is the tear filled eyes and overwhelming feeling I have of thankfulness and gratitude for each and every Confederate soldier that fought and sacrificed; lived or died through the battles and skirmishes. An honor and respect I only have to give in return. I fly that Confederate Battle Flag in remembrance of what it truly stood and still stands for. We can never repay them now for what they did for us then.

If you visit the South you can expect to see the Confederate Battle Flag being sold at roadside stands, like this one in Princeton, West Virginia, circa 2015.

25. SCOTT BOWDEN

Arlington, Texas

No matter the nationality, color, or religion of a person, there is a universally-recognized symbol that transcends culture, borders and language. It is a symbol that ignites the passion of patriots just as it is a symbol loathed by authoritarians who seek its elimination. In the most succinct manner describable, it stands for resistance to tyranny—that symbol is the Confederate Battle Flag.

According to the Left, 19th-Century Southern blacks hated the Confederate Flag and would never have fought for the South. Why? Because "it would have been insuring their own continued enslavement." However, as both C.S. President Jefferson Davis and U.S. President Abraham Lincoln both repeatedly and publicly asserted, "the War was not over slavery." Thus, another anti-South myth is easily destroyed by the Truth. Despite the bold facts of the matter, enemies of the South are still desperately trying to hide all traces of the black Confederate. Fortunately, they have not been able to suppress this particular photo, which shows Andrew Martin Chandler (left) and one of his family's servants, Silas Chandler (right), wearing official Confederate uniforms—full fledged soldiers in the 44th Mississippi Infantry. Armed to the teeth in preparation for the fight against the illicit Northern invaders, such brave young men, white and black, were prepared to face death side-by-side if need be. This type of interracial pairing was repeated hundreds of thousands of times across the South during Lincoln's War. While Dixie's black servants were sometimes ordered to go into battle to accompany white loved ones, just as often they went of their own accord, anxious to put on Confederate gray or butternut, and show "Marse Linkum" who was boss. At least 45 blacks served in Nathan Bedford Forrest's cavalry, men he handpicked and enlisted personally. After years of research I can confidently maintain that as many as 1 million African Americans served in the Confederate military in one capacity or another—five times as many as those who served in the Union military. I base this number not only on extensive decades-long studies, but also on the definition of a "private soldier" by German American Yankee General August V. Kautz, who wrote: "In the fullest sense, any man in the military service who receives pay, whether sworn in or not, is a soldier, because he is subject to military law. Under this general head, laborers, teamsters, sutlers, chaplains, etc., are soldiers." This image is from my book *Everything You Were Taught About African-Americans and the Civil War is Wrong, Ask a Southerner!* Spring Hill, TN: Sea Raven Press, 2016.

26. STEPHEN KELLEY

Denham Springs, Louisiana

Whwhat does the Confederate Flag mean to me? For years it was just the flag my older brother flew in the bed of his truck. It was described as "tacky" or "racist", and, on occasion, "historical." Regardless, it was nothing that a child brought up on cartoons and videos games would give much thought toward.

That changed one summer afternoon in Petersburg, Virginia. My family had spent the day visiting the battlefield. While gazing upon a map in the museum, my father looked down and softly said "we should've won that war." I began wondering where his strong feelings came from.

My investigation began the next evening on a trip to Richmond. A tour of the Confederate White House was being held for Museum of the Confederacy donors. A tour guide let us in when I poked my head through the unlocked entrance. We were unaware it was by "invitation only." Due to this oversight, we joined black-tie guests in a private tour of the house led by renowned historians. Each tour guide had different stories to tell about Jefferson Davis, but they all made one point clear: he did not commit treason. Now I was certain that I had to learn the truth.

Unlike most millennials, I'm not very fond of the Internet. I began collecting books on the subject. I read memoirs written by the soldiers who were there, as well as analyses written in the 21st century. I read everyday for a year, then I finally knew why my father muttered those words.

That flag was carried into battle by the finest army to ever exist; made up of down home Southern boys. The flag is a well preserved representation of the valor and pride these young men felt. Young men from numerous racial and cultural backgrounds filled the ranks. Boys who came from all walks of life. Farm boys with a strong work ethic and college boys with a strong thirst for knowledge. All of them gave up their security to risk their lives for the noble cause of a constitutional government built on Judeo-Christian principles.

These were better men than most people could hope to be today. I have no desire to follow any type of influencer on social media. The men who I strive to be like carried that flag into enemy fire. They were heroes and should rightly be remembered as such.

These boys have fallen victim of a false narrative. The ones who this flag truly belongs to would've been appalled by the racist groups and segregationists of the 20th century that hijacked their banner. These boys, black and white, worked the fields together. Then they sat shoulder to shoulder on railcars ready to face invaders. They would've thought of separate seating on buses or street cars as infantile.

That makes this flag not only a symbol of bravery, but also of unity and brotherhood. The kind of brotherhood we need today more than ever. That is what the flag means to me.

Confederate veterans parading the Battle Flag at a reunion in 1917.

27. STEVE QUICK

Hilton Head, South Carolina

What people choose to believe about the flag is a choice. One can accept the interpretation of entire states, Southern rock and country bands, NASCAR fans, Kappa Alpha fraternities, thousands of reenactors and a century of thoughtful historians.

People can also embrace the interpretation of a few pathetic racists, an insane mass murderer, or an opportunistic civil rights lobby, well amplified by a sympathetic media. Like all choices its says less about the object than it does about the person.

Perhaps only the Irishman can define the shamrock, or a Jew explain the Star of David. Are not Southerners entitled to the same latitude?

Entitled "Our Heroes and Our Flags," this chromolithograph from 1895 memorializes the Confederacy some three decades after the end of Lincoln's War on the Constitution and the American people. Portraits, clockwise from top center: Jefferson Davis, Alexander H. Stephens, Lt. Gen. Thomas J. "Stonewall" Jackson, Gen. Sterling Price, Lt. Gen. Leonidas Polk, Lt. Gen. William J. Hardee, Gen. J. E. B. Stuart, Gen. Joseph E. Johnston, Lt. Gen. Edmund Kirby Smith, Brig. Gen. John H. Morgan, Lt. Gen. Richard S. Ewell, Gen. Wade Hampton, Gen. Samuel Cooper, Lt. Gen. James Longstreet, Gen. Braxton Bragg, Gen. John Bell Hood, Gen. Ambrose P. Hill, and Gen. Pierre G. T. Beauregard. These encircle an image of Robert E. Lee, an equestrian statue, and the Confederacy's four official flags.

28. THOMAS H. MCFARLAND

Louisville, Kentucky

I was born in Kentucky, adopted at age 5. I was raised in Mobile, Alabama and Pascagoula, Mississippi, in the 1960s. It was segregated in those days and the KKK mostly ruled as law. I remember them marching, meeting, and saw burning crosses. My father campaigned for George Wallace when Wallace was still Governor of Alabama. My father would go to meetings with his men friends weekly and he would bring me the little Confederate flags home. I know now they were table dressing for the meetings together. My father was a Mason and I can't say for sure if he was Klan. In those days, grown up business was not talked about or shared with children.

When I turned 18 my father gave me his flags and a Dixie lighter. It was a wind up lighter that played the "Dixie" melody and I remember hearing it nightly as I would drift off to sleep. It was stolen in 2006 along with my truck and all I owned. I really miss that lighter most of all, and I don't even smoke.

I will have to say, I have *always loved* the Confederate Flag. It is part of my Southern heritage and way of life. I think *it is the most beautiful of all flags*. When I look at it daily, since I have 14 on my walls currently, one 5' x 8', over 100 flags in storage, plus 100s of Confederate items, I almost cry.

I wish things were still Old Southern days when God and

Jesus were honored, America was still one nation under God, men had integrity, men were men, women were women, and we liked it that way. I quit my last year of high school to go to Vietnam as a duty to my country and America's people. I came home, was spit on, abortion was, and still is acceptable, God is kicked out of school, the Pledge of Allegiance gone.

I spent 11 years in Clearwater, Florida, 1985, and I can say even today, Florida still loves her Southern heritage and many fly the Confederate flag. Northern transplants don't like the flag but that's ok too. In 1996 I moved to Pigeon Forge, Tennessee, where a lot of the businesses had signs in the windows saying "No Blacks Allowed." Now businesses are run by India. As of 2018 only 3 Motels are America owned and they put that on their signs and make a great profit!

I have spent the last 25 years there and now the crooked government have brought Northern law to teach cops and courts to be crooked and make money doing it. They ran the Indians across into North Carolina to the New Casino, give the Indians a monthly check, a share in Casino funds, and housing. I used to see the Indians selling their blankets, baskets, foods, and things but now, everything is sold in stores and made in China.

One thing you do see still today, Confederate flags *everywhere* and Confederate *everything* in *all* the stores. Tennessee, I believe, will *never* give up her Southern heritage, or Confederate flags. I plan to move back come the first of 2021. I love Tennessee, rich with spring water. Sevierville,

Pigeon Forge, Gatlinburg, won't allow a bus service to *ever* come from Knoxville, Tennessee, because they don't want black crime to come there. You see a few blacks, mostly vacationers, or a very few workers. I love the people there, real country, Southern hospitality and honesty. I think that is what I always loved most about growing up in the South, what I miss in today's world.

I love my Southern heritage, my Confederate Flags, it's not just a tradition, it's home, a way of pure life, a love for God. I will forever fly my flags and I will never give into this world's ways. God says in Romans 12:2, "And be not conformed to this world: but be ye transformed by the renewing of your mind, that ye may prove what is that good, and acceptable, and perfect, will of God."

I am a Vietnam Veteran but, I will never display the American flag. I will stand for it out of honor to my country, to our fallen soldiers and their families, but my home lands are forever Dixie. I never do and never will go north of Kentucky.

Thank you for letting me share my love for my flag of heritage and Southern life. Forever Dixie!

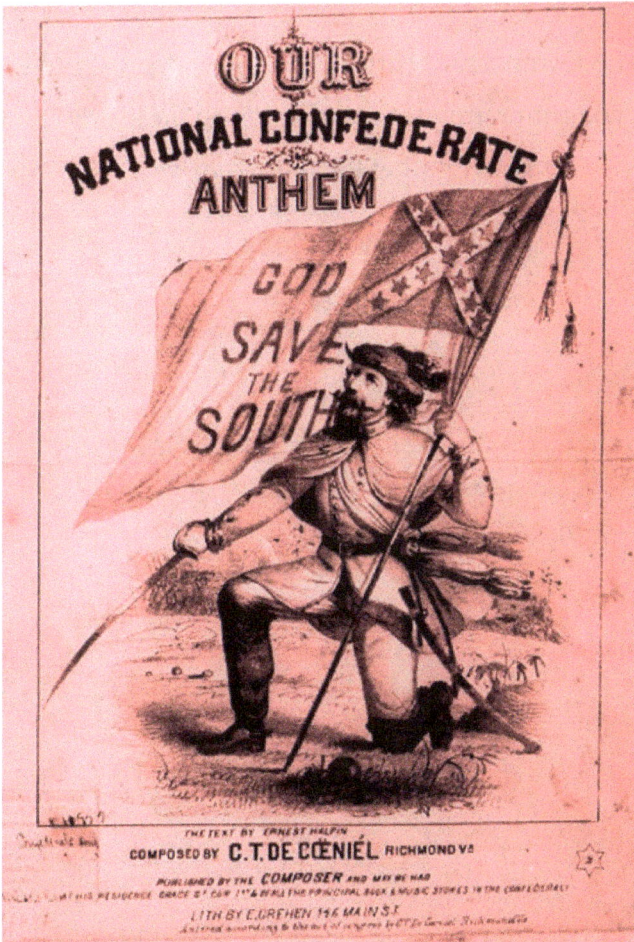

Victorian cover sheet for the Confederate National Anthem: "God Save the South."

29. TOM HAMILTON

Delia, Alberta, Canada

The Confederate Battle Flag is a symbol of pride. And a constant reminder that fighting on the losing team is *not* the same as fighting for the wrong side!

The Confederate Battle Flag has made prominent appearances at marches, protests, and rallies ever since the War for Southern Independence. As a symbol of both the patriotic Conservative South and resistance to totalitarianism, authoritarianism, despotism, dictatorship, socialism, and communism, the flag was quite appropriately seen most recently at support rallies for Right-wing U.S. President Donald J. Trump—in many ways a 21st-Century version of Right-wing C.S. President Jefferson Davis.

30. TOM KOPCZAK

Greensburg, Pennsylvania

I'm a Northerner by birth but a Copperhead by choice. To me, the Confederate battle flag represents freedom and defiance to a tyrannical government. Those soldiers of all races who fought under that flag were defending their homes and family from an invading army, as well as defending the original Constitution of this country.

It is hard for me to imagine that in less than 100 years that government had become so corrupt that Conservatives were left with no option but to secede. I believe that many who vilify the battle flag do so to distract others from learning the truth about the North and Lincoln.

Can you imagine if Lincoln's many crimes came to light? We've built memorials to him, even placed him on our currency. I will continue to display the flag in honor of those brave soldiers.

This photo from about 1909 shows a group of girls waving Confederate flags at a dedication ceremony for a Confederate monument in Mulberry, Tennessee.

31. WESLEY D. KING

Odessa, Texas

From my earliest memories of growing up in oil-rich West Texas, the Confederate Battle Flag has always represented a non-conformist attitude; a sense of "I will be *me*, on *my* terms," with all due respect to Freedom and Liberty. Everyone I know, and have known, understands Southern, conservative, Christian values, which marks us as different and causes us to stand out. We don't look for handouts, we show courtesy and respect to women, we enjoy (and create) good food and good music. Most of the things the PC culture mock and make jokes of us for, we heartedly laugh at as well. Because we true Southerners recognize envy when we see it!

Everything great about the Southern States, known as the CSA, is contained in the image of the Battle Flag. What the world sees as great about America and causes a burning desire to cross oceans to get here—Freedom of Speech, Mrs. Baird's sliced bread, Blue Bell ice cream, Rock & Roll, Country Music, New Orleans Jazz, Wal-Mart, America's Team, SEC Football, Whataburger, Jack Daniels, Tyson Chicken, Mardi Gras, on and on, the brightest artists, the most famous military leaders, the most patriotic, are *all* Southern.

When I see the Confederate Battle Flag, to me it is a symbol of how set apart we are and how proud we are when it is raised—the back drop on an old Lynyrd Skynyrd stage, the top of the General Lee, and at one time throughout the stands at a NASCAR race— it means we enjoy freedom, family, and friends.

After the *Washington Post* ran an article about 2 months before the Charleston Church killings in 2015, stating how America would be more like Europe if it wasn't for the South (which I knew to be a good thing), I began to learn about the War Between the States and the new insistence to purge any truths about the CSA from the public square (literally and figuratively).

Now, more than ever, sons and daughters of Southern ethnicity need to grasp what this Flag means to them and what it means to those against it! One can't be a proud American, celebrating the 4th of July, and believing themselves to be Constitutional Conservatives without smiling proudly when they look at the Southern Cross of our Confederate Battle Flag and defending it. Period.

I pray it's not too late to teach the truths exemplified by the attitude and presence of the Confederate Battle Flag!

This chromolithograph from *Puck* magazine, dated "Memorial Day, 1899," promotes the idea of national unity nearly 40 years after the start of Lincoln's War. Standing beneath a U.S. Flag, on the left is a Confederate soldier, on the right a Union soldier. At the center is a veteran of the Spanish-American War. The caption reads: "Three Veterans Under One Flag."

32. W. G. HARDEMAN

Tennessee

In my opinion, the Confederate Battle Flag represents a message of self government and stubborn resistance to all forms of tyranny. Embedded in the design of the flag is Saint Andrew's Cross, which is of great significance to the historical Celtic roots of the American South. My ancestors have fought and shed their blood under the rallying cry of this banner.

There are two other banners that all honorable Southerners hold in high regard that express this selfsame message: 1. The Bonnie Blue Flag and 2. The Christian Flag, which bears a representation of the Cross of my Commander and Savior, Jesus Christ.

On June 5, 1922, Confederate Memorial Day services were held at Arlington National Cemetery, Virginia. One of the chief guests was U.S. President Warren G. Harding, who spoke before a massive crowd—and a large Confederate Battle Flag—in honor of the Confederate soldier. The Left is attempting to suppress this photo because it counters their fake history about the South and Lincoln's War. This book will preserve it, and the Truth, for all time.

33. WOODY W. WOODWARD

San Antonio, Texas

To me the Confederate Battle Flag represents courage in the face of almost certain death. It represents commitment to country, family, compatriots, brothers, and a belief in God and His promise of everlasting life. It is a symbol of love, honor, and a dedication to adhere to one's duty no matter the cost.

A Confederate Battle Flag made out of flowers highlights the Confederate monument behind it, at Jasper, Alabama, circa 2010. By order of the Confederate Congress' Joint Committee on Flag and Seal, on April 19, 1862, a resolution was issued concerning an earlier but similar Confederate Battle Flag design to the one shown here, declaring that: "The red field denotes nautical powers, boldness, courage, valour. The saltire [the X-shaped diagonal cross], an 'honourable ordinary' in heraldry, is the emblem of progress and strength; its white indicating purity, innocence, and gentleness. The [color] blue . . . represents justice and faith, perseverance and vigilance."

INDEX

Allen, Robert, 97, 98

Amiss, Thomas B., 48

Anneke, Fritz, 87

Baird, Mrs., 122

Barnett, T. J., 31

Beacroft, Percival, 95

Beauregard, Pierre G. T., 7, 16, 57, 62, 113

Benavides, Santos, 139

Benjamin, Judah, 139

Benson, Al, Jr., 39, 40

Boren, Doug, 54, 55

Bowden, Scott, 107

Bragg, Braxton, 16, 113

Bricker, Birch, 42-44

Brown, Ridgely, 146

Brown, Ridgley, Mrs., 146

Bunker, Christopher, 139

Castello, Robert, 100

Chandler, Andrew M., 108

Chandler, Silas, 108

Claxton, W. L., 22

Cleburne, Patrick R., 93

Clinton, Bill, 65

Cooper, Samuel, 113

Cooper, Wade H., 56

Cornett, Rachel, 84

Dana, Charles, 87

Daniels, Jack, 122

David (Bible), 112

Davidson, Gaylord, 56

Davis, Jefferson, 11, 19, 29, 45, 62, 83, 84, 86, 95, 108, 109, 113, 119, 140

Davis, Julia, 90

Davis, Michael, 90

Douglass, Frederick, 137

Easton, B. B., 145

Eaton, Edward O., 50

Edgerton, H. K., 42

Engels, Friedrich, 21

Ewell, Richard S., 113

Fears, Bobby, 49

Fish, Sandra G., 104, 105

Forrest, Nathan B., 18, 29, 45, 62, 84, 108

Gadsden, Christopher, 132

Galloway, W. C., 56

God, 46, 47, 51, 55, 61, 75, 81, 86, 90, 114-117, 127, 140, 143

Gore, Al, 65

Grant, Ulysses S., 45, 56

Hamilton, Alexander, 42

Hamilton, Tom, 118

Hampton, Wade, 113

Hannon, James, 20

Hardee, William J., 113

Hardeman, W. G., 125

Harding, Warren G., 126

Harding, William G., 85

Hewitt, J. H., 96

Hill, Ambrose P., 113

Hood, John B., 16, 64, 113

Jackson, Stonewall, 12, 29, 84, 113, 137, 140

James, Frank, 57

James, Jesse, 57

Jefferson, Thomas, 19, 42

Jent, Elias, Sr., 84

Jesus, 80, 81, 85, 86, 115, 125

Johnson, Chuck, 51, 52

Johnson, James, 66, 67

Johnston, Joseph E., 15, 16, 113

Kautz, August V., 108

Kelley, Stephen, 109, 110

King, Martin L., 43

King, Wesley D., 122, 123

Kopczak, Tom, 120

Kruizenga, J. Sanford, 73

Lander, Frederick W., 20

Lee, Robert E., 16, 20, 29, 45, 84, 88, 113, 143, 145

Lee, Timothy S., 20

Levi (Bible), 102

Lincoln, Abraham, 11, 19, 20, 25, 26, 29, 31, 45, 62, 83, 84, 86, 89, 97, 108, 113, 120, 124, 126, 132, 140, 142

Longstreet, James, 113

Luna, Gil, 60, 61

Marschall, Nicola, 79

Marx, Karl, 19, 21, 25, 26, 89

McFarland, Thomas H., 114-116

McKellar, Kenneth, 56

McKinley, William B., 56

Merritt, Patrick W., 92, 93

Miles, William P., 16, 18, 79

Miller, Kevin J., 63, 75, 76

Morgan, John H., 113

Mosby, John S., 85

Nelson, Louis N., 139

Newsom, Gavin, 42

Nicoli, Carlo, 41

Orwell, George, 26, 28

Parker, Kimberly, 78

Parsons, Mosby M., 16

Peebles, David, 63
Peoples, Elizabeth W., 63, 64
Peoples, George W., 63
Peoples, William H., 63, 64
Peoples-Elam, Gloria, 63, 64
Pierce, James, 69
Polk, Leonidas, 113
Prather, Jason, 71
Prendergast, Joseph, 132
Price, Gary, 57, 58
Price, Sterling, 113
Quick, Steve, 112
Reid, B. L., 46, 47
Rosa, Robert, 87
Rucker, Edmund W., 85
Saint Andrew, 16, 39, 57, 73, 80, 85, 86, 95, 102, 125, 139
Saint James, 83
Saint Patrick, 18
Sawyer, C. C., 96
Schluchter, Kurt, 80-82
Schurz, Carl, 87
Schwartz, Robert M., 102
Seabrook, Lochlainn, 8, 15, 16, 19, 21, 23-26, 28-32, 42, 84-88, 147
Sharp, E. V., 96
Shelby, Joseph O., 16

Sherman, William T., 57, 58
Simon Peter, 80
Smith, Edmund K., 113
Smith, Orren R., 79
Starnes, Clark R., 94
Stephens, Alexander H., 11, 29, 62, 85, 113
Stuart, Jeb, 113
Swan, William G., 85
Taylor, Richard, 16
Terry, Benjamin F., 64
Thompson, C. F., 96
Tompkins, Sally L., 83
Toombs, Robert, 62
Trescot, William H., 41
Trump, Donald J., 65, 119
Wallace, George, 114
Washington, George, 63, 64
Washington, J. T., 64
Washington, Jeremiah, 64
Watie, Stand, 139
Waud, Alfred R., 68, 135
Weber, Max, 87
Willich, August, 87, 89
Woodward, Woody W., 127

The Confederate Battle Flag was not the Confederacy's first flag symbolizing Conservative resistance to Left-wing tyranny. On November, 8, 1860, exactly four months before the Confederacy had even been officially formed, Georgia adopted a resolution to hold a state secession convention. The occasion? The election, a mere two days earlier, of the widely detested big government Liberal Abraham Lincoln, an event that triggered a Southern revolt and impassioned talk of withdrawing from an increasingly socialistic U.S. government. The approval of the declaration was celebrated on that night at Johnson Square, Savannah, where excited crowds gathered to listen to fiery speeches on the many benefits of separation (pictured above). In the darkness, with fireworks exploding in the air, a great bonfire lit up the side of the park's obelisk, upon which hung "the first flag of independence in the South." Emblazoned with a menacing image of a coiled rattlesnake, the upper half contained the words: "Our Motto Southern Rights, Equality of the States." Along the bottom of the banner were the words: "Don't Tread on Me." The banner was created, in part, by Joseph Prendergast, who patterned the design on a much earlier anti-tyranny Southern ensign: the bright yellow Gadsden Flag, named after Christopher Gadsden of South Carolina—an early champion of American independence, a brigadier general in the Continental Army, and a state representative at the Continental Congress in 1774.

Keep Your Body, Mind, & Spirit Vibrating at Their Highest Level

YOU CAN DO SO BY READING THE BOOKS OF

SEA RAVEN PRESS

There is nothing that will so perfectly keep your body, mind, and spirit in a healthy condition as to think wisely and positively. Hence you should not only read this book, but also the other books that we offer. They will quicken your physical, mental, and spiritual vibrations, enabling you to maintain a position in society as a healthy erudite person.

KEEP YOURSELF WELL-INFORMED!

The well-informed person is always at the head of the procession, while the ignorant, the lazy, and the unthoughtful hang onto the rear. If you are a Spiritual man or woman, do yourself a great favor: read Sea Raven Press books and stay well posted on the Truth. It is almost criminal for one to remain in ignorance while the opportunity to gain knowledge is open to all at a nominal price.

We invite you to visit our Webstore for a wide selection of wholesome, family-friendly, well-researched, educational books for all ages. You will be glad you did!

Five-Star Books & Gifts From the Heart of the American South

SeaRavenPress.com

This artist's rendering of two Confederate veterans raising a Confederate Battle Flag is from one of four medallions dedicated to Mississippi history. In 1935 all four were painted inside the central dome of the Mississippi State Capitol at Jackson.

SAVE THE SOUTH

How You Can Help Protect Our Priceless Heritage

LOCHLAINN SEABROOK

☞ CONFEDERATE ORGANIZATIONS: Join a Confederate or Southern heritage preservation organization. There are groups for men, women, and children.

☞ CONFEDERATE HOLIDAYS: Honor your Southern heritage by recognizing important Confederate holidays and dates, as well as the birthdays of Confederate officers, soldiers, martyrs, heroes, and heroines. Although the South has numerous official Confederate holidays you can celebrate, feel free to create your own around Confederate people, events, and days that are personally important to you and your loved ones. Turn them into annual festivities that your family looks forward to.

☞ OLD SOUTH HOSPITALITY: Practice Old South social customs: Avoid gossip, refrain from swearing in public, smile at strangers, make eye contact while conversing, hold the door open for others. Saying "yes ma'am," "please," and "thank you," never goes out of style. All are part of the famous hospitality that has such deep roots here in Dixie.

☞ SOUTHERN WISDOM: Pass along your Southern wisdom, knowledge, and experience to your children and grandchildren.

☞ SOUTHERN ETIQUETTE: Teach youngsters the conservative ways of Southern social etiquette, such as table manners, graciousness, humility, and respect for elders.

Artist Alfred R. Waud drew this pencil sketch depicting "the 1st Virginia Cavalry at a halt" around September 1862. The 13 star Confederate Battle Flag is prominently displayed.

☛ FAMILY CUSTOMS: Transmit your family's customs to your progeny. If your parents hunted and fished, played the fiddle, clogged, made jams, or worked on cars and trucks, teach these activities to the next generation.

☛ HOMESCHOOLING: Homeschool your children in order to prevent them from being indoctrinated by our pro-North, South-hating, communist influenced public school system.

☛ YOUR SOUTHERN LINEAGE: If your family is originally from the South, rest assured you have a prestigious, honorable, and patriotic American lineage: no matter where you live or what your race, you almost certainly had ancestors who sided with the Confederacy or who fought in the Confederate military during the War for Southern Independence. This makes you special: you are a descendant of a Confederate soldier, or at the very least a Confederate family, something every educated individual should be proud of!

Besides the 1 million European Americans who donned Confederate gray, some 300,000 to 1 million African Americans, 70,000 Native Americans, 60,000 Latin Americans, 50,000 foreigners, 12,000 Jewish Americans, and 10,000 Asian Americans, all served in the Confederate army and navy in one capacity or another. According to former Yankee slave Frederick Douglass, Stonewall Jackson's army alone contained some 3,000 fully armed and trained black soldiers.[21]

---

21. For more on these and related topics see my book, *Everything You Were Taught About the Civil War is Wrong, Ask a Southerner!* 2010. Franklin, TN: Sea Raven Press, revised 2019 ed.

Completely contrary to what our Leftist South-loathing media and government want us to believe, the Confederate Battle Flag is loved, admired, idolized, cherished, respected, treasured, exhibited, and flown in all 50 states, as well as in countries in every part of the globe. In fact, happily, interest in and support for the Confederate Flag (that is, what she stands for) is increasing exponentially every year worldwide—particularly in the U.S. This 2018 photo is of a tent vendor in Florence, Oregon.

☛ OUR MULTIETHNIC HISTORY: Whatever your race or ethnic background, if your ancestors were Southern, appreciate your heritage and declare it publicly. This is yet another way you can help reeducate the inculcated masses while preserving our heritage.

As all traditional Southerners are aware, though the C.S.A., or Confederate States of America, was created by people of European and primarily Christian background (hence the Saint Andrew's Cross on our national and military flags), the creation and evolution of the South herself was shaped by people of all races and colors, including African, Spanish, Native American, and Asian.

Blacks, for instance, have been in the Americas since the late 1400s, and in North America since the early 1600s, far longer than many white Southern families.[22] As such, African influences played a large role in the development of Dixie, contributing to everything from Southern architecture and gastronomy to Southern music and language, characteristics that remain strongly evident in the 21st Century.[23]

Non-Christians, such as Jewish Confederate Secretary of War Judah Benjamin, and non-whites like Indian General Stand Watie (of the 1st Cherokee Mounted Rifles), Hispanic Colonel Santos Benavides (commander of the 33rd Texas Cavalry Regiment), Asian Christopher Bunker (of Co. I, 37th Battalion, Virginia Cavalry), and African American Private Louis Napoleon Nelson, of the 7th Tennessee Cavalry, Company M. (the only known black Confederate chaplain), are five more examples of the broad racial,

---

22. For more on the history of early African Americans, particularly in the South, see my book, *Everything You Were Taught About American Slavery War is Wrong, Ask a Southerner!* Spring Hill, TN: Sea Raven Press, 2015.
23. For more on the role of African Americans in shaping the South see my book, *The McGavocks of Carnton Plantation: A Southern History - Celebrating One of Dixie's Most Noble Confederate Families and Their Tennessee Home.* 2008. Franklin, TN, 2011 ed.

ethnic, and religious makeup of the Confederate government and military.

☞ CONFEDERATE CHRISTIANITY: While many strong Christian Confederates were very liberal in their approach to Christianity (General Stonewall Jackson, for example, allowed men of any Christian denomination to preach and lead camp prayers), the Confederate States of America was a Christian-based government. Thus, whether a Confederate supporter is a Christian or not (note that I have met several Confederate atheists), practicing and extolling Christian values is yet another way one can help preserve our Confederate heritage.[24]

The Christianity at the root of the Confederate States of America is in stark contrast to the overt lack of Christianity at the foundation of the United States of America. For instance, the C.S. Constitution includes the word "God," the U.S. Constitution does not;[25] the C.S. National Flag contains a Christian Cross, the U.S. National Flag does not; Confederate States President Jefferson Davis was a devout Christian (Episcopalian), United States President Abraham Lincoln was an atheist (or at the least an anti-Christian agnostic).[26] This list could by multiplied many times.

☞ CONFEDERATE PROSELYTIZING: Take every opportunity to discuss the Confederate Flag, as well as the Confederacy and Lincoln's War, with others. Keep the truth alive.

---

24. For more on General Jackson see my book, *The Quotable Stonewall Jackson: Selections From the Writings and Speeches of the South's Most Famous General*. Spring Hill, TN: Sea Raven Press, 2012 Sesquicentennial Civil War Edition.

25. For more on the C.S. Constitution see my book, *The Constitution of the Confederate States of America Explained: A Clause-by-Clause Study of the South's Magna Carta*. Spring Hill, TN: Sea Raven Press, 2012 Sesquicentennial Civil War Edition.

26. For more on Lincoln's atheism and hatred for the Bible and Christianity see my book *Abraham Lincoln: The Southern View*. 2007. Franklin, TN: Sea Raven Press, 2013 ed.

Confederate soldier atop a Confederate monument at Norfolk, Virginia. In his right hand he holds a sword, in his left he holds aloft the Confederate Battle Flag.

"We do not want or expect Yankees to stop honoring their Union ancestors, and they should not want or expect we Southerners to stop honoring our Confederate ancestors." — Lochlainn Seabrook

☛ CONFEDERATE FLAGS: Fly and display Confederate flags wherever and whenever possible. Keep people accustomed to seeing them. Show the world, and especially the Left, that you are proud of your Southern heritage and that we, along with our fetching awe-inspiring banner, are here to stay.

☛ MY BOOKS: Lastly, read my books on the Confederacy and recommend them to others.

Why is it so vital that we save the South?

Our Confederate ancestors were a courageous, well-schooled, charitable, patriotic, and independent-minded group of people. Just think, they were willing to sacrifice everything, their homes, businesses, health, even their lives, for a mere idea. And that idea was *Americanism!*

At the base of Americanism is the U.S. Constitution, a unique conservative document that was intended to serve the citizens of what the Founding Fathers called a "Confederate Republic"—that is, the U.S.A. When the Left-wing North began overturning the Constitution (to we Southerners our country's most important document), Dixie rightly felt she had little choice but to leave the Union. And so, in reluctantly parting ways with her former Northern colleagues, the Southern people formed their own republic, calling it, after one of the early nicknames for the U.S.A., the "Confederate States of America," or C.S.A.[27]

This perfectly legal action was illegally denied by Liberal Lincoln, who promptly and unconstitutionally sent 75,000 Yankee invaders into a constitutionally formed foreign country (the C.S.A.)

---

27. For more on these topics see my book, *Confederacy 101: Amazing Facts You Never Knew About America's Oldest Political Tradition.* Spring Hill, TN: Sea Raven Press, 2015.

to further suppress the rights of the Southern people.

Tragically, General Robert E. Lee's army (though not the entire South) was eventually worn down by a better funded and better equipped foe many times its size. Nonetheless, the Southern Cause—that is, Americanism, or in modern parlance, Conservatism (which includes the constitutional guarantee of states' rights)[28]—did not die out with the South's capitulation on April 9, 1865. It thrives today like never before in the hearts and minds of Conservatives; not only in the American South, but all across both the U.S. and around the world. Indeed, some of my most ardent and loyal readers live in the American Northeast as well as in foreign countries from every part of the globe.

In honor of the many sacrifices our Confederate ancestors made in their attempt to preserve the Founders' original Constitution, and in order to perpetuate the conservative foundation upon which our confederate republic was built, let us forever honor their names, memories, and deeds. As this very book pointedly illustrates, this can be accomplished, in great part, through the preservation of all that it means to be traditionally Southern: love of God, family, and country.

In the future, as the Truth is increasingly and more widely

28. See Amendments 9 and 10 of the U.S. Constitution, where states' rights are tacitly assured.

dispersed, more Confederate flags will be flown, new Confederate organizations will be formed, more Confederate holidays will be created, additional Confederate cemeteries will be consecrated, more Confederate books will be written, new Confederate art and music will be produced, and new Confederate statues will be erected. L.S.

The End

A Confederate Veterans Reunion, circa 1917, at the White House, Washington, D.C. The Confederate Battle Flag is being carried by someone in the back, just visible to the lower left of the "Tar Heels" banner. A C.S. veteran at the front of the parade proudly shoulders a Confederate First National Flag.

As "Commander-in-chief of all Confederate states armies," no one in the South is more closely identified with the Confederate Battle Flag than Robert E. Lee. Thus, if one wants to truly understand the Southern passion for our flag, one must first understand Lee: who he was, what he stood for, and what he fought for. Entitled "In Memoriam Genl. Robert E. Lee," this engraving shows a portrait of the great Confederate chieftain surrounded by the four official Confederate government flags. The text below Lee reads: "The Pure Patriot. The Chivalrous Soldier. The Sincere Christian. The Type of All That is Noble in Man. Born Jan'y 19th, 1807. Died October 12th, 1870. To the Officers & Soldiers of the Confederate Army, His Companions in Arms, This Tribute to His Immortal Worth Is Respectfully Inscribed. Macon, GA. B. B. Easton. Sic Semper Tyrannis." The obelisks on either side are inscribed with some of Lee's more important battles and engagements. From left to right: Gaines Mill, Malvern Hill, Sharpsburg, Chancellorsville, Wilderness, Cold Harbour, White Oak Swamp, 2nd Manassas, Fredericksburg, Gettysburg, Spotsylvania C. H., Petersburg." On the front face at the base of each obelisk is a rectangular box with the letters "REL" inside. For more on this most remarkable human being see my books: *The Quotable Robert E. Lee* and *The Old Rebel*.

A United Confederate Veterans Reunion at Ford City, Alabama, circa 1924.

"Real history is extremely complex. Thus, good historians approach it like a brain surgeon: slowly, methodically, and delicately. Bad historians are like lumberjacks." — Lochlainn Seabrook

Mrs. Ridgley Brown, probably the wife of Lieutenant Colonel Ridgely Brown of Co. K, 1st Virginia Cavalry Regiment, holding an 11-star First National Confederate Flag.

MEET THE AUTHOR

NEO-VICTORIAN SCHOLAR LOCHLAINN SEABROOK, a descendant of the families of Alexander Hamilton Stephens, John Singleton Mosby, Edmund Winchester Rucker, and William Giles Harding, is a 7th generation Kentuckian and the most prolific pro-South writer in the world today. Known by literary critics as the "new Shelby Foote" and by his fans as the "Voice of the Traditional South," he is a recipient of the prestigious Jefferson Davis Historical Gold Medal. As a lifelong writer he has authored and edited books ranging in topics from history, politics, science, religion, astronomy, and biography, to nature, music, humor, gastronomy, genealogy, and the paranormal; books that his readers describe as "game changers," "transformative," and "life altering."

One of the world's most popular living historians, he is a 17th generation Southerner of Appalachian heritage who descends from dozens of patriotic Revolutionary War soldiers and Confederate soldiers from Kentucky, Tennessee, North Carolina, and Virginia. A proud member of the Sons of the Confederate Veterans, he began life as a child prodigy, later transforming into a true Renaissance Man. Besides being an accomplished and well respected author-historian and Bible authority, he is also a Kentucky Colonel, eagle scout, screenwriter, nature, wildlife, and landscape photographer, artist, graphic designer, songwriter (3,000 songs), film composer, multi-instrument musician, vocalist, session player, music producer, genealogist, former history museum docent, and a former ranch hand, zookeeper, and wrangler.

His (currently) 78 adult and children's books contain some 60,000 well-researched pages that have earned him accolades from around the globe. His works, which have sold on every continent except Antarctica, have introduced hundreds of thousands to vital facts that have been left out of our mainstream books. He has been endorsed internationally by leading experts, museum curators, award-winning historians, bestselling authors, celebrities, filmmakers, noted scientists, well regarded educators, TV show hosts and producers, renowned military artists, esteemed heritage organizations, and distinguished academicians of all races, creeds, and colors. Colonel Seabrook holds the world record for writing the most books on Southern icon Nathan Bedford Forrest: 12.

Of northern, western, and central European ancestry, he is the 6th great-grandson of the Earl of Oxford and a descendant of European royalty. His modern day cousins include: Johnny Cash, Elvis Presley, Lisa Marie Presley, Billy Ray and Miley Cyrus, Patty Loveless, Tim McGraw, Lee Ann Womack, Dolly Parton, Pat Boone, Naomi, Wynonna, and Ashley Judd, Ricky Skaggs, the Sunshine Sisters, Martha Carson, Chet Atkins, Patrick J. Buchanan, Cindy Crawford, Bertram Thomas Combs (Kentucky's 50th governor), Edith Bolling (second wife of President Woodrow Wilson), Andy Griffith, Riley Keough, George C. Scott, Robert Duvall, Reese Witherspoon, Lee Marvin, Rebecca Gayheart, and Tom Cruise.

A constitutionalist and avid outdoorsman and gun advocate, Colonel Seabrook is the author of the international blockbuster, *Everything You Were Taught About the Civil War is Wrong, Ask a Southerner!* He lives with his wife and family in beautiful historic Middle Tennessee, the heart of the Confederacy.

For more information on author Mr. Seabrook visit

LOCHLAINNSEABROOK.COM

Our flag is here to stay.

If you enjoyed this book you will be interested in Colonel Seabrook's other popular related titles:

☛ ABRAHAM LINCOLN WAS A LIBERAL, JEFFERSON DAVIS WAS A CONSERVATIVE
☛ EVERYTHING YOU WERE TAUGHT ABOUT THE CIVIL WAR IS WRONG, ASK A SOUTHERNER!
☛ ALL WE ASK IS TO BE LET ALONE: THE SOUTHERN SECESSION FACT BOOK
☛ EVERYTHING YOU WERE TAUGHT ABOUT AMERICAN SLAVERY IS WRONG, ASK A SOUTHERNER!
☛ CONFEDERATE FLAG FACTS: WHAT EVERY AMERICAN SHOULD KNOW ABOUT DIXIE'S SOUTHERN CROSS
☛ LINCOLN'S WAR: THE REAL CAUSE, THE REAL WINNER, THE REAL LOSER

Available from Sea Raven Press and wherever fine books are sold

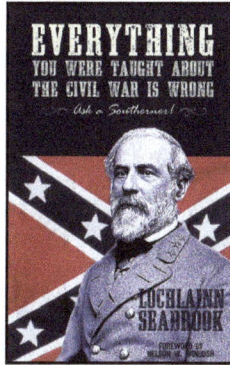

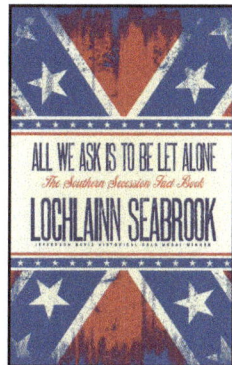

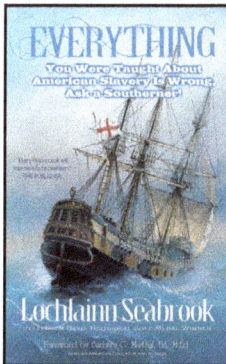

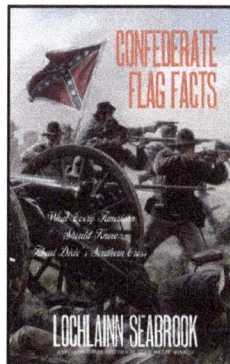

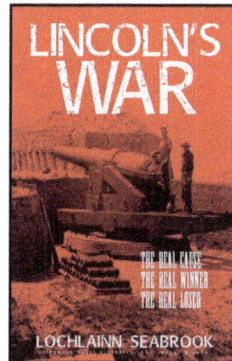

SeaRavenPress.com